Cambridge Elements

Elements in the Renai

edited by

John Henderson
Birkbeck, University of London, and Wolfson Coll
Jonathan K. Nelso
Syracuse University Florence, and Kennedy School, Harvard University

THE WORLD IN DRESS

Costume Books across Italy, Europe, and the East

Giulia Calvi
University of Siena and European University Institute

Shaftesbury Road, Cambridge CB2 8EA, United Kingdom

One Liberty Plaza, 20th Floor, New York, NY 10006, USA

477 Williamstown Road, Port Melbourne, VIC 3207, Australia

314–321, 3rd Floor, Plot 3, Splendor Forum, Jasola District Centre, New Delhi – 110025, India

103 Penang Road, #05–06/07, Visioncrest Commercial, Singapore 238467

Cambridge University Press is part of Cambridge University Press & Assessment, a department of the University of Cambridge.

We share the University's mission to contribute to society through the pursuit of education, learning and research at the highest international levels of excellence.

www.cambridge.org
Information on this title: www.cambridge.org/9781108823302

DOI: 10.1017/9781108913829

First published 2022

A catalogue record for this publication is available from the British Library.

ISBN 978-1-108-82330-2 Paperback
ISSN 2631-9101 (online)
ISSN 2631-9098 (print)

The World in Dress

Costume Books across Italy, Europe, and the East

Elements in the Renaissance

DOI: 10.1017/9781108913829
First published online: August 2022

Giulia Calvi
University of Siena and European University Institute

Author for correspondence: Giulia Calvi, Giulia.calvi@eui.eu

Abstract: In the early modern period, costume books and albums participated in the shaping of a new visual culture that displayed the diversity of the people of the known world on a variety of media including maps, atlases, screens, and scrolls. At the crossroads of early anthropology, geography, and travel literature, this textual and visual production blurred the lines between art and science. Costume books and albums were not a unique European production: in the Ottoman Empire and the Far East, artists and geographers also pictured the dress of men and women of their own and faraway lands, hybridizing the Renaissance Western tradition. Acknowledging this circulation of knowledge and people through migration, travel, and missionary and diplomatic encounters, this Element contributes to the expanding field of early modern cultural studies in a global perspective.

Keywords: dress, knowledge, global, material culture, Renaissance

ISBNs: 9781108823302 (PB), 9781108913829 (OC)
ISSNs: 2631-9101 (online), 2631-9098 (print)

Contents

1 Staging the Clothing of the Early Modern World

Preface

Beginning in the mid-sixteenth century, printed collections of clothing circulated in Europe, gaining a widespread success on the editorial market. They contained engravings of various size, which quickly became objects of curiosity, amusement, and decoration. While more than 200 of these books circulated in Europe between 1520 and 1610, production increased most perceptibly after 1550 in Paris, Venice, and Nurnberg, the most prominent centres for publishing (Tuffal, 1955; Olian, 1977).[1] The historiography that mostly focusses on European costume books agrees on some basic assumptions that identify dress as the category which in the early modern period structured a discourse on social, cultural, and gender difference. Alongside portraits, costume books were the new medium expressing individuality in a visual format, which projected the author's experience of the urban space in terms of habitat, work, and commerce. Research has also highlighted the visual culture these editorial productions shared with Renaissance chorography and cartography, as maps of cities and continents were often decorated with the dress of local inhabitants, reinforcing the connection between dress and place. Space became visible through the images of men and women wearing local attire. Recent studies have highlighted references to travel literature, botanical illustrations, and emblem books, all of which also shaped the visual apparatus of costume books (Ilg, 2004; Wilson, 2005; Mentges, 2007; Rublack, 2010).

In the early modern period, the equation of the gendered body with dress and civic space is in tension with a widening notion of space in terms of exploration and conquest and the construction of a non-Western, non-Christian other. Costume books staged the bodies of men and women on an ordered theatre of the world, displaying the most visibly evident components of otherness. Abraham Ortelius with his atlas, *Theatrum Orbis Terrarum* (1570), translated into Dutch (1571), German and French (1572), and Spanish (1588), and in 1606 into English as *The Theatre of the Whole World*, disseminated the figure of the world theatre across Europe. The title invited readers to comprehend the world both as a whole and through its local representations by experiencing an imaginary voyage displayed on the page. In a similar way, costume books invited readers to delve into human diversity on a micro level through the clothed bodies displayed on the theatre of the world and contained in a book (Riello, 2019: 284).

[1] One of the first books is Francois Deserps, *The Various Styles of Clothing*. A facsimile of the 1562 edition, Sarah Shannon, ed. (Minneapolis, MN: James Ford Bell Library, 2001).

In the context of growing curiosity and knowledge about non-Western peoples and lands, costume books comprised multifaceted notions of dress. An inclusive representation of dress as the bodily practice of combining nudity and bodily manipulations – tattoos, foot bondage, sexual mutilation – was in tension with the traditional meaning of costume, one that the Renaissance imbued with ethical and gendered notions of moral conduct, and with fashion as a sign of change and modernity in Western societies. Recent research recommends looking at the body as a 'strategy' for thinking about the global. In the context of world history, bodies are embedded in processes of circulation, mobility, exchange, and trade, providing, as it were, the basic connection of global interactions (Burton, 2012). In their fanciful attires, the people of the world displayed in costume books embodied abstract notions of space, suggesting to the readers ideas about distance and proximity, place, climate, ethnicity, sexual identity, and age. At the crossroads of early anthropology, travel literature, and visual culture, costume books blurred the lines between art and science. The clothed and naked bodies of men and women appearing on a variety of media (chorographies, atlases, world maps, costume albums and books, screens) partook in the early modern construction of a humanized global space where gender, ethnic, language, and religious differences prevailed over skin colour.

The early modern texts analysed in this Element communicate to readers from the twenty-first century a gaze that is astonished and yet free of a consolidated Western superiority. It is a gaze shaped by classical antiquity, travel diaries and missionary accounts, and the often derivative and imaginary pictures of clothing portrayed in drawings, engravings, and books that proliferated throughout Europe.

Until recent years, historians rarely questioned the normative monopoly of the Western gaze in defining and fixing the representation of world peoples via images, literature, and geographical, anthropological, and clinical investigation. However, global contacts and encounters offered other people the opportunity to describe, represent, and hybridize the (European) foreigners arriving in the lands they inhabited. Ethnographies therefore were not only a Western production, though Europeans 'enjoyed asymmetric advantages in that they were able to compile a much more comprehensive body of global cultural knowledge than any other people' (Bentley, 2011: 8).

The Circulation of Knowledge in and beyond Europe

The three sections of this work show how compendiums, travelogues, visual sources, missionary reports, and cartography were crucial to the elaboration of images and texts in Italian, European, and non-Western costume albums and books. All three sections acknowledge the circulation of books, prints, and maps through agents (merchants, scientists, diplomats, missionaries, artists, travellers) across Europe and between East and West. Information not only travelled from the West to the Far East, but, as Sections 2 and 3 show, in the other direction as well. My central argument focusses on the circulation and translation of culture in costume books and albums across global connections. Images were traced and texts were copied and at times translated into images, spurred by an editorial market eager for plates that depicted people nobody had ever seen (as, for example, the Arctic population in northern Scandinavia before the 1550s, the Japanese in Europe before 1582, or the Portuguese in Japan before the 1540s).

Costume books were not a unique European production: in the Ottoman Empire and the Far East, artists and geographers pictured the dress of men and women of their own and faraway lands in manuscript albums, scrolls, and prints. Analysing these sources in non-Western contexts is another crucial contribution this Element intends to make to the expanding field of early modern global cultural studies. Addressing a growing readership in Japan or a European audience in Turkey, costume albums produced in Istanbul and Tokyo are also considered in tension with the Renaissance Western tradition. Structured on synthesis, repetition, and accumulation, these tracts develop a discursive model increasingly grounded on difference, in an expanding world unknown to biblical and classical sources. Costume books represent others through the lens of power, status, religion, trade, ethnicity, gender, and age. They address a readership attracted to exotica in a widening market of luxury goods where foreigners are becoming part of the domestic landscape (Bleichmar, 2011: 15–30; Bleichmar and Mancall, 2011). A startling desire for information is perceivable in most of them, the desire to know about foreigners and where they come from as well as a troubling anxiety about otherness and others.

The following paragraphs focus on the Venetian artist Cesare Vecellio's two editions of his *Habiti antichi e moderni* (*Ancient and Modern Clothing*) in the context of map-makers, geographers, and the printing trades in the cosmopolitan society of the late Renaissance.

The Ancient and Modern Clothing of the World

Cesare Vecellio (1521–1601) authored the largest and most important Italian costume book representing the peoples of the world. It was printed in Venice in two editions: *Degli habiti antichi e moderni di diverse parti del mondo* (1590) and *Habiti antichi e moderni di tutto il mondo* (1598). While the first edition pictures the clothing of the three continents (Europe, Asia, Africa), the second one includes the New World and represents the four continents. The two editions are illustrated with 428 woodcuts (1590) and 503 woodcuts (1598) provided by Christopher Chrieger, a German printmaker whose name was Italianized as Cristoforo Guerra.

In recent years, much has been written on Cesare Vecellio, a versatile artist, active as a painter, engraver, and printmaker living and working in Cadore, Belluno, and Venice in the second half of the sixteenth century. The *Habiti* are the most extensively discussed costume books by Renaissance specialists mainly in terms of a history of clothing, textile production, and dress which is now expanding in the field of global fashion studies (Wilson, 2005; Jones and Rosenthal, 2008; Paulicelli, 2008; Paulicelli and Clark, 2009; Riello and McNeil, 2010; Riello, 2019). Sidestepping the analytical perspective of a history of fashion, my methodological approach to Vecellio's costume books is that of viewing them as a 'contact zone' (Pratt, 1992) where a wealth of visual and textual sources is creatively appropriated and reinterpreted. In this framework, addressing the circulation of knowledge and cultural translation, the *Habiti* appear to be a dynamic genre situated in a changing geopolitical context shaped by Western and non-Western cross-cultural exchanges. This methodological approach informs the three sections of this Element, which focus on three different contexts: the Scandinavian peninsula, the Ottoman Empire, and Japan. Venice as a global city (Wilson, 2005) and a printing centre provides connections between a situated local knowledge and cross-cultural exchanges across Italy, Europe, and the East.

Born in Pieve di Cadore in 1523, Cesare was a distant cousin of Tiziano Vecellio and was trained in his workshop in Venice, where the large Vecellio household cooperated under the artistic direction of Tiziano himself. Owing to a lack of sources concerning his life, Cesare was unacknowledged as an artist in his own right, and it was only in 1817 that Stefano Ticozzi in his *Vite dei pittori Vecellij del Cadore* mentioned Cesare as a close collaborator of Tiziano's (Ticozzi, 1817). Giovan Battista Cavalcaselle, in his famous monograph on Tiziano (1878), listed some works which he attributed to Cesare, whose contribution could be distinguished from that of other family members in the master's workshop (*bottega*). However, subsequent studies did not shed light on any documents concerning Cesare's life and work or his relationship to Tiziano. Only a few quotes in the 1590 *Habiti* mention a trip to Augsburg in 1548, where the artist and his collaborators were invited to paint a portrait of Charles V and his court. After Tiziano's death in the Venetian plague of 1576, Cesare probably received part of the drawings, etchings, and sketches as well as some of the precious textiles listed among his belongings. Carpets and woven patterns appear in Cesare's paintings in the 1580s and 1590s and recent historiography from the Cadore has suggested a connection between these new motifs and Tiziano's legacy (Guérin Dalle Mese, 2002; Tagliaferro and Aikema, 2009).

In the 1570s, Cesare painted a series of portraits of a family from the local uprising nobility, the Piloni. Count Odorico, head of the household and holding important political charges, became his patron and friend. In his palace near Belluno, the count, Vecellio wrote, 'has a study. In addition to many kinds of books, this study is full of every ancient object one could desire, including ancient medals, portraits of heroes, and marble and bronze sculptures, as well as wondrous natural artifacts in substances of every noble kind. Throughout the region it is called Noah's Ark' (Vecellio, 1590: 219; Rosenthal and Jones, 2008: 271). The artist decorated the volumes of Piloni's precious collection of books with hand-coloured miniatures of exotic landscapes and imaginary portraits on the edgings, to make it look like a gallery of paintings rather than a library. Many of the Renaissance bestsellers that Cesare perused and quoted in his *Habiti* came from Piloni's library in Belluno. It is important to acknowledge the tension between the local embeddedness of the count as a jurist, politician, and major collector and the transnational update of his library and Wunderkammer – a key feature of the intellectual world of Venice and its mainland and of the transfer of knowledge and communication across Europe.

Vecellio's work was part of a well-connected world of engravers, printers, artists, and cartographers such as Giacomo Franco and Pietro and Ferdinando Bertelli who engraved costume books as well as maps (Woodward, 1996, 2007; Bury, 2001). Venice became a leading printing centre because of its trade networks, its political autonomy, and its tradition of freethinking. Beginning in the early sixteenth century, a growing entrepreneurial class of government officials, artisans of the metal and paper trades, merchants, and intellectuals provided a fertile ground for the spreading of the new technology and connected lay and church intellectuals with a wider readership for whom knowledge of the wider world was no longer a luxury but a necessity. Vecellio had his own smaller printing business and printed maps. Texts and images thus represent the clothed inhabitants of the world through the prism of the artist's contextualized reading of space. A keen awareness of the changing space of the world shapes the *Habiti*: a wealth of sources combines references to paintings, monuments, and tombstones with a large body of geographical and historical knowledge circulating in Venice from the mid-sixteenth century.

Gendering Civic Culture and Global State Power

A systematic comparative reading of the two editions underlines some crucial differences that are central to the argument presented in this Element. The first *Habiti* (1590) mainly addresses a local Venetian readership, is entirely written in Italian, and consists of two books, one dealing with the European dress of men and women and the other dealing with the costumes of Asia and Africa in the framework of the old three-continent partition of the world. Each illustration is set in an elaborate frame and is flanked by a page providing a detailed description of the image, from the top of the engraving down. Vecellio began with the hairstyle or headdress, worked his way down over the shoulders to the bust, arms, and hands, and ended with the feet. He detailed textiles, patterns, colours, and accessories – gloves, fans, handkerchiefs, flowers. He then explained how the individual costume was used, on what occasion and by whom, and to what extent the fashion was popular. Shaped by the Renaissance tradition of portraiture, the culture of self-fashioning and the use of models, costume books have been compared to emblem books or to collections of botanical engravings in which each plant species is presented singly, divided by genus on distinct plates set one next to the other (Wilson, 2005). This iconographic approach oriented towards analogy was useful in presenting the masculine and the feminine in both the natural and the human worlds.

Vecellio's explicit intent was to delineate a history of clothing and thus to provide a documented history of the images on the woodblock prints: he traced their origins from paintings, tombstones, frescoes, or books, or from news spread by travellers landing in Venice. Political and social power shape the artist's gaze that focusses on hybrid styles of clothing in colonial territories such as Venice's Stato da Mar. Religion is one of the key features distinguishing attire among the Protestants, Christian Orthodox, Jewish, Armenian, and Islamic people, and ritual – especially the bridal marriage dress – grants ethnic continuity of customs and costumes for minorities. Most of the genealogy of ancient and modern clothing in the first *Habiti* (1590) deals with women's fashion, and the female body played the greatest role in giving shape to the theatre of the world. The first edition features a culture of civic urban virtues in which noblewomen have a prominent visual position and female costumes embody some European cities, regions, and kingdoms.

The second edition (1598) is written in Latin and Italian, addresses a cosmopolitan readership, and is divided into twelve books comprising the peoples of Europe and of the world (including North and South America) within the modern four-continent division of the world. The prose loses all reference to local scales of representation and knowledge as well as to individuals.

Adopting a rather generic descriptive quality acquired through a systematic reduction of texts, the prose is mostly confined to a short description of the costume, eschewing information about customs and contexts. Here the images are set within a global history of costumes and customs. Princes with their royal gowns and insignia systematically move in, substituting the female icons of civic virtue in favour of a representation of state power embodied by men, which develops into a male-centred visual construction of global space. Adding America with twenty new prints was the crucial step in this direction (Van Groesen, 2008). Information had to be updated as the earth was no longer perceived to be made up of empty spaces surrounding familiar places and faces but was recognized as fully and densely inhabited by unknown men and women (Headley, 1997; Hodorowich, 2005).

As shown in Section 3, two new plates picturing the costumes of the Molucca Islands and Japan embodied the space of the Pacific and were the key to the global dimension of the second edition of the *Habiti*. It indeed staged the costumes of the whole world connecting the four continents through the written and visual sources that agents – diplomats, missionaries, travellers – brought with them. Migrations, diasporas, and the transfer of people and material culture provide the larger framework for the transcontinental circulation of images and texts that this Element illustrates.

The leading Italian, French, and German costume books, as well as the bestsellers that in the mid-sixteenth century appeared on the European book market and their Italian editions, mostly printed in Venice, shaped Vecellio's *Habiti*: Ramusio's collection *Navigazioni e Viaggi*, Olaus Magnus' *Historia de gentibus septentrionalibus*, Nicolas de Nicolay's *Navigationi et viaggi*, Juan Gonzales de Mendoza's *Historia de la China*, and De Bry's *Collection of Voyages*.

Cesare Vecellio died in 1601. He was eighty years old and had survived the devastating 1576 plague that hit Venice and northern Italy. He published the first edition of the *Habiti* at sixty-seven and completed the second at seventy-five, a very old artist leaving behind him the world in a book.

The 'New World Within'

Passing from the first to the second edition, Vecellio modified the boundaries of Northern Europe, introducing new peoples – the inhabitants of Scandia (Scandinavia) – and calling it the 'new world in Europe'. The definition came from Giovanni Botero, a Jesuit scholar who between 1591 and 1597 was completing his encyclopedic *Relazioni Universali* (Botero, 2015), a masterpiece of Western and Catholic universalism offering armchair travellers a global tour around the four continents. Writing about the northern peninsula bordering the ocean to the west and the north and the Baltic Sea to the south and the east, Botero defined it as a new world because it was inhabited by so many different peoples. Huge whales, monsters with human heads, and enormous quantities of fish were part of a wondrous landscape that nevertheless suggested commercial opportunities as herrings, salmon, and precious furs created trading networks and attracted capital. Both Vecellio and Botero compared Stockholm to Venice. The city where the king of Sweden resided was – like Venice – 'built in the marshes on wooden poles. The sea enters in two branches so deep and large that ships loaded with merchandise arrive with full blown sails' (Vecellio, 1590: 329; Botero, 2015: 202). For Italian readers, the new and the unknown were framed in a familiar context.

None of the European authors of costume books – Bertelli, De Bruyn, Boissard, Grassi, Weiditz – from whom Vecellio had copied many images had gone so far as to include the hyperborean regions or the inhabitants of the last Thule. Only the Venetian Pietro Bertelli had designed a Finnish costume, but on the whole Italian culture continued to depend on what it could glean from the work of the *auctores* who, in medieval times, had dominated in the field of geographical and encyclopedic studies (De Anna, 1988, 1994). In Venice, Ramusio had printed the travelogues of Pietro Querini, who had been shipwrecked near the Lofoten Islands in 1432. The reports from the envoys from the Holy See, at the forefront those of Antonio Possevino written between 1577 and 1580, remained inaccessible and locked within the Roman archives of the Curia and then of the Jesuits. The Arctic was the totally unknown, the void, and what was surprising to many Renaissance thinkers, it was missing from ancient sources. In this sense it was a new world and another world within Europe.

Recent historiography has connected the invisibility of the Far North in sixteenth-century sources to the ways in which Arctic exploration took place. Early modern Arctic encounters were a largely Protestant phenomenon and Dutch and English explorers shared their cultures' anxiety about the theological value of images – sculptures, paintings, handcrafted figures – as leading to idolatry (Heuer, 2019). The Dutch Jan Huygen von Linschoten's 1594–5 voyage to Lapland is a meaningful example of his identification of local sculptures with threatening idols. Arctic works appeared in a time of violent iconoclasm and religious wars when the traditional Christian conceptions of the image were being challenged. The invisibility of the last Thule, wrapped in ice, fog, darkness, and sorcery, suited the iconoclastic ideology of Northern European explorers who assimilated this landscape to the Reformation's attacks against idols in the Netherlands, Switzerland, Germany, and France. The Far North became a contact zone where religious zealots fought their culture wars verging on the meaning of visuality.

Olaus Magnus, *Historia de gentibus septentrionalibus*

In this context, it was not by chance that Olaus Magnus (1490–1557), the Swedish archbishop of Uppsala, authored the most imaginative and densely illustrated encyclopedic tract on the northern peoples, *Historia de gentibus septentrionalibus*. He was concretely involved with the Reformation debate over the moral and religious use of pictorial art at the Council of Trent, taking an uncompromising stand against iconoclasm. It was in Trent, where he appeared as a stranger from unknown lands, that he started planning his colossal history of the Far North 'numbed by the constant merciless cold' (Olaus Magnus, 1565: pp. 1–2; Heuer, 2019). In the foreword of his *Historia*, Olaus glorifies pictorial art as 'poetry without words [which] in its harmonious use of lines, colours, proportions, and in its imitation of living objects' preserves the memory of the past, inspires honourable deeds, and is a *magistra vitae* full of delights (Johannesson, 1991: 168). He wrote and reproduced in 480 woodcuts the first detailed description of the people of Scandinavia in their wondrous natural environment. Owing to Olaus' militant opposition to the Protestants' iconoclasm, Scandinavia appeared to Renaissance readers in a wealth of images (Gillgren, 1999).

Olaus Magnus is one of the great and, at the same time, perhaps one of the least known figures of Renaissance cultural history. Born in Linkoping in 1490, between 1519 and 1521, he wandered across Norway with his brother Johannes, who was made the archbishop of Uppsala in 1521. Because of his duties for the church and the king, he travelled widely in Sweden, Norway, and northern Finland. When Lutheran-friendly forces under Gustav Vasa conquered Stockholm in 1523, both brothers went into exile, travelled incessantly through Europe, and lived for long periods in world cities such as Danzic, Venice, and Rome. In Venice in 1539, Olaus published a maritime map of Scandinavia under the auspices of the Venetian patriarch Geronimo Quirini. The *Carta marina* printed with two informative booklets in Italian and German was full of wonderful illustrations of monsters, battles, and shipwrecks, of reindeers pulling chariots over icy rivers and lakes, hunters, and missionaries. It had a wide diffusion and its vignettes were repeated in the *Historia de gentibus septentrionalibus*. It was considered the most accurate map of Scandinavia (Miekkavaara, 2008).[2] However, the *Carta* and the *Historia* did not only offer

[2] For a colour reproduction of the *Carta marina*, see http://hornorkesteret.wordpress.com/2010/01/18/olaus-magnus-carta-marina-1539.

a wealth of illustrations: as we shall see, they were embedded in the conquering ideology of the Catholic Counter-Reformation (Lestringant, 2005: 6).

The brothers settled in Rome in 1541 in the Swedish hospice of Saint Birgitta, today in the piazza Farnese. Both died in Rome, Johannes in 1544 and Olaus in 1557. The latter was named archbishop in his brother's place but never returned to Sweden. He attended the first Council of Trent between December 1546 and March 1547 and conceived of his monumental *Historia de gentibus septentrionalibus*, where he depicted the north not just as a fragmented landscape of ice and darkness, but as a potentially promising region in terms of natural resources worthy of reconquest by the papal forces.

Upon his return to Rome in 1547, Olaus installed two printing presses in the hospice of Saint Birgitta and employed an émigré from Parma to work them. The encyclopedic *Historia* shaped by the classics (especially Pliny), northern folklore, personal observation, and experience, generously illustrated with 480 woodcuts, was printed in Latin in Rome in 1555. Translations in French (1561), Dutch (1562), Italian (1565), German (1567), and English (1658) followed. It was not published in Swedish until 1909. In his own country, Olaus Magnus was a controversial figure who embodied the last generation of Catholic bishops opposing Gustav Vasa's conversion to Protestantism, the requisition of monastic property, and state-building – all of which Swedish historiography identified with modernity. A vast and seemingly unmanageable encyclopedia, full of fantasies with no scientific grounding, in Sweden the *Historia* was discredited and forgotten. It was better known in abridged editions, called *epitomes*, circulating among European scholars across confessional lines.[3] Olaus' sources for the images included his brother's *History of the Gothic and Swedish Kings* that was published in 1554, Hans Holbein's prints of the Old Testament, and Ariosto's *Orlando Furioso* in Gabriele Giolito's 1549 edition. It seems probable that Olaus first produced sketches himself but left it to his Italian engraver to complete his pictures (Johannesson, 1991: 163–70). These were the only images of the Scandinavian peninsula and of the Arctic region circulating in Renaissance Europe.

The Indigenous Populations of Lapland and Biarmia

To the Southern Europeans to whom the book was addressed, the icy new world was upsetting because of the monstrosities it contained – whales, snakes, giants,

[3] The *Historia* comprises twenty-two books The first books describe the climate and geography. The author then moves on to describe warfare and peace in Scandinavia. In the second part of the work, Olaus discusses at length the animal kingdom, beginning with mankind and ending with insects. The twenty-two books supposedly mirror the structure of the Old Testament with its twenty-two books and perhaps even Augustine's *City of God.*

demons – and because of its spiritual depravities – paganism among the Lapps and the Lutheran heresy. Olaus turned the Lapps, forced to pay rising taxes by the Swedes and the Norwegians, into the good savages of the Far North. He expressed his concern for 'The Lapps who live in faraway wild spaces. They are very little known and do not use money, but barter whatever they need. They live together without conflicts, in peace, without envy nor fraud' (Olaus Magnus, 1565: 115). They speak a strange language, pay tributes to the king of Norway and to the prince of Muscovy under whose rule they are obedient subjects, and offer their ministers precious furs. They marry, baptize their children, and bury their dead with rituals that hybridize Christian ceremonies with the Indigenous devotion for fire. Olaus believed that the nomadic people of the Far North would be fully converted to Christianity were it not for the distance between their dwellings and the churches and the heavy taxes in precious furs they were forced to pay to the Swedish king. In Italy, Botero, in his *Relazioni Universali*, worded similar concerns about the religious situation in Scandinavia and the conversion of the Indigenous populations of Lapland and Biarmia still tied to their pagan heritage, to divination, sorcery, and shaman culture. He probably read Olaus Magnus, but, as many authors at the time did, avoided quoting his sources. Botero writes:

> They are small but agile and dress in tight clothing. In winter they wear the skins of sea cows or entire bearskins. They tie them to their heads leaving only an opening for the eyes – this has given some writers a cause to report that they are as hairy as animals. They have no homes but live in tents as the Tatars. Instead of horses, they have reindeers. They also have huge bears and very white ermines. Their furs attract foreign money. The Biarmi live like the Lapps: they adore fire, they revere magic, and they fill the air with spells. They are subjects of the king of Sweden. (Botero, 2015: 202)

Olaus Magnus' defense of the Lapps against the oppressive fiscal policy of the Swedish kings intersects in new ways recent Swedish postcolonial historiography that analyses the role of material culture in enforcing a colonial order in the land of the Sami in northern Norway, Sweden, Finland, and the Kola peninsula in north-western Russia – Lapps and Biarmi in the sixteenth century (Nordin and Ojala, 2018). According to this recent research, the 'othering' of the Indigenous population anticipated the destruction of its religion, language, and material culture. Beginning in the seventeenth century, collections of Sami material culture constructed a dominant Western view of the population and served as a local variant of the colonial collections in the making of European empires. Renaissance authors such as Damiao da Gois in his *Deploratio Lappianae Gentis* (1540) and Olaus Magnus in his *Historia* (1555), albeit within Catholic universalism, contributed to compare the Indigenous populations of Scandinavia to those of America. Frank Lestringant underlines the analogies between Olaus' pleading for the Lapps and the Dominican Bartolomé de Las Casas' defence of the Indians (Lestringant, 2005: 3).

Dressing Northern Men and Women: Cesare Vecellio and Olaus Magnus

Research has brought to light very limited connections between Olaus Magnus' monumental work and sixteenth-century Italian culture. Only the poet Torquato Tasso (1544–95) mentioned the *Historia* in his tragedy *Il Re Torrismondo* (1587). It opens with a reference to Biarmia, the region in the north of Finland that inaugurates book I of the *Historia*. Tasso quotes whole passages almost word for word, operating an esthetic integration of Olaus within Italian literature (Wodianka, 2015: 33). But the Far North was made visible also through the selection, appropriation, and reinterpretation of the *Historia*'s impressive visual apparatus. To date the wealth of images – 480 woodcuts – that Olaus Magnus circulated in Italy and Europe has not attracted the attention of scholars, yet they did not go unnoticed in sixteenth-century Venice. Cesare Vecellio included twenty-four woodblock prints that embody the new world of the Far North in his *Habiti antichi e moderni di tutto il mondo* (1598): twelve are dedicated to women and twelve to men. Among these, the most visually powerful represent the men and women from Biarmia, Scrifinia (Finland), and Lapland. They derive from Olaus Magnus' *Historia delle genti et della natura delle cose settentrionali* (1565), which was indeed the only sixteenth-century source on the inhabitants, the environment, and the customs of the Scandinavians.

Translated from Latin and printed in Venice by Giunti, the *Historia delle genti et della natura delle cose settentrionali* was the product of a network of artists, engravers, and printers that included Vecellio's workshop and small printing business. The artist was acquainted with Olaus' work and already in the first *Habiti* (1590) he quoted passages from book XIV, chapter V, which dwell on the marriage ritual among the simple folk in the Baltic islands south of Sweden. He transcribed whole sentences but did not use the images.[4] The layout of the first *Habiti*, with its long descriptive texts detailing local history and traditions, fitted well the ethnographic dimension of Olaus' *Historia*, where clothing was a minor part of the narrative and where contexts and environment were a crucial aspect of the encyclopedic volume.

[4] In the first edition, a couple of illustrations of the Swedish bride and matron and of the women from the Baltic islands are scattered among others portraying German, Dutch, Polish, and Swiss dress.

Eight years later, in Vecellio's second *Habiti*, images overwhelmed the text, reduced to a few sentences in Italian and Latin. The lengthy ethnography of dress was eschewed from the narrative and the images acquired greater prominence. The north gained a visual coherence and images migrated, as it were, from Olaus to Cesare. In so doing, they changed drastically, moving from a rather sober representation of couples and households to the individual portraits that Vecellio drew in the Renaissance tradition. Lapps, Finns, and Biarmi were isolated from their human and natural environment and set inside single frames decorated with grotesques that domesticated their wild appearance into the canons of classical and Italian visual traditions. Following the suggestions of recent postcolonial critics, I argue that Vecellio put on display the peoples of the Scandinavian Arctic, both *othering* them and *Westernizing* them. In so doing, he introduced the costumes of the unknown inhabitants of Scandinavia to the readership in Southern Europe.

It took Vecellio eight years to select, draw, engrave, and print the new images that he derived from Olaus. He assembled them with the costumes from Sweden, Muscovy, and the Baltic islands which he had already included in the first edition. He also elaborated some of Olaus' prints into imaginative and appealing plates that the Venetian printer Giunti probably cherished (Del Puppo, 2011). Through these complex intellectual choices that shaped the new book VI, the clothing of the new world within Europe was selected, reinterpreted, integrated, and given visual continuity within the *Habiti* as a global project.

Material Culture and Everyday Life

In the following pages, the texts and images of the two works by Olaus Magnus and Cesare Vecellio are compared for the first time, focussing on the latter's selection and transformation of the original source and on the new meanings the images acquired, migrating, as it were, from an encyclopedic ethnography of peoples and their physical environment to a costume book.

Material culture and everyday life figure prominently in the opening chapters of the *Historia*. Olaus introduces the reader to northern Finland and its inhabitants, who walk at great speed because they wear 'flat long wooden shoes with their points arched upwards' made according to men and women's heights (Olaus Magnus, 1561, I, III: 4). Figure 1 shows three hunters on skis with a dog in pursuit of a reindeer and a wolf. Two tents suggest the nomadic life of the population and fur clothing is also enhanced.

Vecellio repeats the text, adding a synthetic description of men and women 'used to hunting all sorts of wild animals across mountains and cliffs dressed in the furs of bears, wolves and other animals. That's what they mainly live off'

Figure 1 Olaus Magnus, *Historia* (1565) *Man and woman from Finland*[5]

(Vecellio, 1598: 295). In the *Habiti*, a woodblock print pictures a couple: the man and the woman are dressed in fur and wear long skis (Figure 2). Vecellio eliminated the third hunter, the dog, the wild animals, and the tents. As in the original, the couple is shown hunting with bow and arrow in a simplified, barren landscape of rocks and snow. All reference to nomadism is lost.

The Venetian artist added another plate on the clothing of the Finns (Figure 3) with a short text emphasizing the great physical strength, simple dress, and the equality between the genders. 'These sorts of men and women are trained to hunt in childhood and to face all sorts of strenuous endeavors. They dress in fur and their arms are wrapped in deerskin. They carry a stick that helps them to go into deep valleys and cliffs pursuing all sorts of animals' (Vecellio, 1598: 296). The text and image epitomize the long descriptions in the *Historia* and make them easily accessible for readers.

Darkness was one of the key features of the Nordic climate that authors insisted upon. The enduring night of the long winter months fills Olaus' narrative and communicates fright and loss to the reader. Olaus delves into dark forests, night battles, and voyages. Chapter XIV in book II is dedicated to night travels. In it, Olaus pictures a man travelling during the night and using the mushrooms growing on the rotten bark of oak trees to produce light, just like fireflies – also in the vignette – do in summer (Olaus Magnus, 1565, II, XIV: 46) (Figure 4).

Vecellio repeats the image under the heading *Northern men travelling* (Figure 5). He separates the man from the lively landscape of trees, river, fireflies, and houses, but reproduces objects, dress, and posture and adds a short description

[5] I have translated all captions from Italian in Olaus Magnus, *Historia delle genti et della natura delle cose settentrionali* (1565) and Cesare Vecellio, *Habiti antichi e moderni di tutto il mondo* (1598).

Figure 2 Cesare Vecellio, *Habiti* (1598) *Man and woman from Scrifinia.* The Berenson Library, Villa I Tatti

of the traveller's dress: 'made of heavy cloth with deerskin trousers. He wears a fur hat with a very long visor. During such travels, they carry an axe, a crossbow, and arrows' (Vecellio, 1598: 292). The visual narrative of the original source is lost.

The bark of trees was also used in domestic settings, to shed light on everyday tasks. 'At home they use candles of pine wood that are naturally full of resin,' comments Olaus. 'They keep a handful of such candles tied to the waist and, if their hands are busy, they carry a lit one in their mouth' (Olaus Magnus, 1561, II, XV: 47) (Figure 6).

The plate shows a man and a woman at home with torches in their mouths so as to keep their hands free. The room, possibly a kitchen, has a fireplace and windows. The man seems to be coming in from outside, and he is carrying a jug

Figure 3 Cesare Vecellio, *Habiti* (1598) *The clothing of Scrifinia*. Berenson Library, Villa I Tatti

and a basket. The woman holds a spindle and has pinewood candles tied to her belt. A dog sleeping in the background highlights the cosy domestic setting.

Vecellio uses the image and the text in his print on *Women from the north* (Figure 7). He isolates the woman both from the domestic setting and from the man and adds a commentary suggesting to Venetian readers that women who are busy with the spindle and who carry their own wooden candles do not come from the élite:

> In the North, women from the lower orders usually carry some wooden sticks tied to their belts. They burn like candles as one can see in the portrait. Their dress is long, of thick cloth, and they wear an apron from which hangs a small bag with needles. On their heads they wear the linen that they spin outdoors. In their mouths they carry a wooden candle that makes light. (Vecellio, 1598: 290)

Figure 4 Olaus Magnus, *Historia* (1565) *Journeys in darkness*

Figure 5 Cesare Vecellio, *Habiti* (1598) *Northern men travelling*. Berenson Library, Villa I Tatti

Figure 6 Olaus Magnus, *Historia* (1565) *About lighting and torches*

Figure 7 Cesare Vecellio, *Habiti* (1598) *Women from the north*. Berenson Library, Villa I Tatti

The print of the woman from the north shows how the artist selected the image, isolating it from the original context and transforming it into a framed portrait. The plate thus fitted the layout of the costume book, where attention to dress both as a signifier and as a signified is the key. Vecellio assumes the clothing from the original and then describes it in the accompanying text. His gaze captures posture and gestures, as well as the texture and materiality of leather, fur, and cloth that seem to be mostly colourless.

Two powerful imaginary portraits inspired by Olaus picture the man and woman from Biarmia, in the north-east of Finland, close to the Arctic pole (Figures 8 and 9). 'The night is six months long and so is the day in summer,' Vecellio comments, describing the man's fur, skis, and heavy hat that covers his ears. He carries a saber, crossbow, and lance. His figure is imposing in contrast

Figure 8 Cesare Vecellio, *Habiti* (1598) *Man from Biarmia*. Berenson Library, Villa I Tatti

Figure 9 Cesare Vecellio, *Habiti* (1598) *Woman from Biarmia*. Berenson Library, Villa I Tatti

to the descriptions found in other sixteenth-century tracts which mention the short height of these people (Botero, 2015, 1: 202).

Dynamically placed on the edge of a cliff and ready to shoot, 'women from *Biarmia*' – writes Vecellio – 'just like their men, enjoy fishing and hunting. They are monstruous and engage in sorcery and magic. They dress in fur and leather, and they wear a pair of ornamental horns on their hat. They are skilled archers. Their stockings and shoes are like those of their men' (Vecellio, 1598: 294). In book III, Olaus dedicates a long description to divination and magic among Finns, Laps, and Biarmi. Deep in trance, their shamans fall to the ground and cast spells to fight faraway enemies whose strength is thus drained from their bodies. Among these peoples, women practise sorcery and black magic using their everyday pots and pans to prepare magic concoctions, boiling herbs, mushrooms, worms, and guts. They thus attract who they want, but they also make people sick and die. They look wild and go hunting and are often better hunters than the men. They also catch many sorts of birds and use the most tender feathers for their beds. The tougher feathers are used to construct handlooms. With feathers, they also make hats, caps, and head ornaments (Olaus Magnus, 1561, III, XIV: 96; IV, XII: 126–7).

Vecellio includes an imaginary portrait of a man from Lapland: his hat, leggings, and coat down to his knees are made of precious furs; he holds a bow and arrow in his hands (Figure 10). His feet are strangely naked. 'Not all wear precious furs and some dress in heavy cloth according to their status' (Vecellio, 1598: 297).

In contrast to what Olaus writes about these Arctic nomads who wear precious furs out of need and not vanity (Olaus Magnus, 1561, III, XIV:

Figure 10 Cesare Vecellio, *Habiti* (1598) *The clothing of Lapps*. Berenson Library, Villa I Tatti

114), the Venetian artist underlines the social differences highlighted by clothing. Furs were a marker of status and a sign of luxury in Europe and beyond, and sumptuary laws prohibited men and women, except for courtiers, from wearing the furs mentioned in the book on northern clothing. The appropriation and resignification of the image addressed Venetian readers who were well aware of such regulations and identified fur with luxury and not with the need to protect oneself from the harsh climate of the Scandinavian peninsula.

Christianization and Marriage

Precious furs also decorated bridal costumes, and marriage is a central feature of the *Historia*. In Olaus Magnus' view, Catholic marriage – instituted by the decrees of the Council of Trent – as a bulwark against Protestantism, Russian Orthodox Christianity, and idolatry – was the key for the assimilation of Scandinavia to civilization. In the first *Habiti* (1590), Vecellio had quoted detailed passages from the Scandinavian wedding ceremonies among the lower orders, repeating Olaus' painstaking description of the careful choice of a bride and bridegroom from Christian parents, the ritual performed in the parish church with witnesses and the consensus of the young couple, the ring, and the priest's final blessing (Vecellio, 1598: 371–2). Outside the church, a group of young men staged a *charivari*, a remnant of folk traditions. Olaus described step by step the ceremonies of the wedding, leading to the priest singing the hymn *Veni creator spiritus* before the marital bed. The following day, the bride poured exquisite wine in silver goblets to signal she has 'already become a mother' (Olaus Magnus, 1561, XIV, V: 341–3).

Vecellio added to this long passage a print picturing the *Bride from Livellandia* derived from the Frenchman Jean Jacque Boissard's costume book (1581) as Olaus did not provide any suitable image and Vecellio had not completed the northern costumes for his second edition. Eight years later, in book VI of his global *Habiti* (1598) where Lapps and Biarmi play a prominent role, the Venetian artist adds an imaginary portrait of a bride from Lapland (Figure 11). 'She wears the finest ermine and sable clothing and a leaf shaped fur hat. The sleeves are large, and the shoes are long following the custom of the country. Brides ride to their husband's home on a reindeer and are in the company of many people, depending on their noble status' (Vecellio, 1598: 298). The text is brief and focusses on the dress. Only the reference to the bride riding a reindeer comes from Olaus.

In contrast to Vecellio's extremely synthetic text, Olaus provides a detailed ethnography of the Lapps' marriage customs, according to status and ethnicity.

Figure 11 Cesare Vecellio, *Habiti* (1598) *The bride from Lapland.* Berenson Library, Villa I Tatti

Following the narrative pattern he used for Scandinavia, he dwells on the norms regulating the selection of spouses, the marriage rituals, the payment of the bride price, and the exchanges of gifts. The Christianization of Scandinavian society was not uniform, and Olaus observed with great attention the syncretistic practices, as well as the resistance to the adoption of the Catholic wedding. The violent kidnapping of a virgin was still a wedding practice among the peasant Muscovites, Ruthenians, Lithuanians, and Livonians, and, moving to the north and the east, the areas in which Christianization – and therefore civilization – did not occur became greater. The Lapps perform weddings with fire produced by striking a stone with iron, because they believe that the outward sign of the true union of man and wife is like that between fire and stone, and 'even the more civilized Christians in the north celebrate their weddings with fire,' he commented. After the celebration of the wedding with the ritual of fire, the Lapps put the bride, dressed in ermine and sable furs, on the back of a reindeer, and, in the company of many people according to the nobility of her lineage, she rides to her husband's home. The husband 'wears marten and lynx fur as if he dressed in the clothes of a Venetian gentleman, and walks behind' (Olaus Magnus, 1561, IV, VII: 119). The somewhat ironic parallel between Laps and Venetians is quickly inverted as Olaus observes that the value of Scandinavian furs is much higher than that of silk gowns and golden chains, emphasizing the commercial opportunities offered by the north's natural resources. Fire is at the heart of Scandinavian ritual, and the sacredness of light infuses Christian ceremonies: baptisms and funerals are conducted by the light of torches brought into the church and blessed. After giving birth, women also 'go to Church with lit torches' (Olaus Magnus, 1561, IV, VII: 118–19).

Women play a dominant role in Olaus' and Vecellio' s representations of northern peoples. Gender equality is a distinguishing feature of society in the Arctic zone, where women are pictured hunting in the wilderness and living in tents. Like the men, they fish, run on ice with their skis, and practise magic. Beginning in late antiquity, this became a *topos*, as the devil supposedly resided in the Far North and encouraged the spreading of sorcery, seducing women. In opposition to the genderless pattern prevailing in the wild and its dehumanizing effects, the Christian bride and mother pave the way to change, acting as intermediaries in the civilizing process through the institution of Catholic marriage and the formation of a Christian family.

Olaus insists on the difficulty of Christianizing people who live in forests far away from churches and of baptizing their children.

> [C]ompassionate [C]atholic priests preached the gospel to these wild people and converted them to the Christian faith but it is impossible to convert all of them because they are so isolated and far that they rarely can come to church. However, those who become Christians obey their priests and their bishops and manage to go to church once or twice a year to baptize their children. They carry them in baskets that they tie to their backs where they also put the precious furs they offer their priests in payment for their tithes.
>
> (Olaus Magnus, 1565, IV, XVI: 131)

Figure 12 shows a couple from Lapland, both carrying two children on their backs, distributed according to gender: the father brings two boys and the mother two girls. The children are miniatures of their parents and wear similar caps and hats. The couple has reached the end of the journey, travelling on skis, and has arrived at the church. They are dressed in fur and carry sticks.

Figure 12 Olaus Magnus, *Historia* (1565) *On christening of children among forest dwellers*

Vecellio repeats from Olaus the text and woodcut, following the usual pattern of isolating a single figure from the context and translating it into a portrait. He eliminates the man and the church and focusses on the mother. The text also describes only the mother carrying her children in a basket and points to the 'extravagant' hat shown in the image. The children in the basket are naked (Vecellio, 1598: 299).

Both authors give ample space to women, stressing the tension between the genderless social model prevailing in the Arctic wilderness and the gendered Christian model of the wife and mother. Magnus viewed Christianization through Catholic marriage as the key to civilization in these largely unexplored lands and Vecellio integrated this ideological approach into his costume book (Figure 13). The choice of the *Historia* as the main source for picturing and integrating the northern others was not a merely aesthetic one, nor was it neutral: Archbishop Magnus provided hundreds of images because he was a Catholic and a militant opponent of Protestant iconoclasm at the Council of Trent. His images were therefore loaded with ideology, the same one Vecellio complied with as an artist.

As Sections 2 and 3 show, religion as a main component of difference and identity on a global scale was crucial in shaping the representation of the costumes and customs of the world, not only in Western albums, but also in the Turkish and Japanese albums and books that are overviewed in the following pages.

Figure 13 Cesare Vecellio, *Habiti* (1598) *Northern Christian woman*. Berenson Library, Villa I Tatti

2 The Ottoman Empire

An album with the drawings of costumes that Cristoforo Roncalli, Il Pomarancio (1552–1626), made for his patron, Vincenzo Giustiniani, at the beginning of the seventeenth century is the starting point for Section 2. To date, Pomarancio's album has never been studied or published, and it is the point of entry into the main questions this section addresses: the relation between patrons and artists; and the sources, meaning, functions, and connections of albums and costume books.

Expanding into a broader framework, the analysis turns to the circulation of albums and books beyond Europe, across the Ottoman Empire and its multiethnic and multireligious visual and textual traditions. Plates depicting the clothing of men and women in two colonial contexts – the island of Chios and the Stato da Mar, Venice's eastern Mediterranean dominions – point to the visual agency of Latin and Orthodox Christian minorities among Islamic populations, outlining the importance of dress as a marker of ethnicity, language, religion, and status.

The section then explores the making of costume albums in the Ottoman Empire, mostly in Istanbul from the sixteenth century to the eighteenth. It outlines the changing art markets targeting a European and Ottoman clientele and the hybrid visual juxtapositions that the format of costume albums disseminated. The album with its experimental layout underlines cross-cultural interaction and connections among urban centres and new consumers. Its parallel developments in Europe, the Ottoman Empire, and the Far East point to a changing consciousness of space and spatial relations in the early modern era, highlighting several questions that relate to early modern globalization.

A Painter, His Patron, and an Album of Drawings

Cristoforo Roncalli, whose nickname was Il Pomarancio – from Pomarance, a town close to Pisa, where he was born – was an important proto-baroque painter (Ambrosini Massari, 2017). He made a 'book of clothes from different nations' comprising 106 black-and-white watercolour drawings while travelling with his patron, Marchese Vincenzo Giustiniani (1564–1637), across the north of Europe in 1606. The manuscript frontispiece introduces the reader to the layout of the drawings: 'On each page he designed figures dressed in the different clothes he saw in different countries with an incredible intelligence and ease' (Gabinetto dei Disegni e delle Stampe [GDS], Roncalli Cristofano, *Disegni di Figura dal 2968 al 3062*, Frontispiece).[6] During the trip, the artist also made

[6] The frontispiece bears the following title: Cristoforo Roncalli delle Pomarance, 'Libro d'abiti di diverse nazioni'. The album measures 36 x 25 cm.

other sketches, 'to remember landscapes and various things', but his drawings of buildings and landscapes are lost – only the costume album survives (Chiappini di Sorio, 1983).

Pomarancio was active in Rome, in the papal entourage, and in central Italy. He was president and then rector of the important Accademia di San Luca de i Pittori e Scultori di Roma (Saint Luke Academy of Painters and Sculptors in Rome). His patron, Vincenzo Giustiniani, a wealthy banker, art theoretician, and owner of one of the most remarkable collections of ancient and modern art – in his Roman *palazzo*, he displayed thirteen Caravaggios – met Pomarancio in Osimo (Feci, Bortolotti, and Bruni, 2001). The artist had signed a contract to decorate the cupola of the local duomo and had started to work on the frescoes (Haskell, 1980: 29–30; Chiappini di Sorio, 1983). Giustiniani was getting ready to leave for a long trip across Northern Europe and invited Pomarancio to join the convoy: he would make drawings of the most remarkable sites, architectures, and landscapes, and discuss the private collections and pictures they visited. Preparing to head to Venice and then across the Alps to the north, Giustiniani offered the artist complete travelling equipment, including a horse and suitable clothing. On his return from this long and rather unusual grand tour, Giustiniani 'had the broadest and most deeply experienced artistic culture of any man in Rome and indeed Europe – with the single exception of Rubens' (Haskell, 1980: 30).

Giustiniani's secretary and friend Bernardo Bizoni was part of the convoy, and he recorded in a diary the most distinguished and colourful events of the voyage, which lasted five months (Bizoni, 1942). The trip – from Italy across Germany and the Low Countries to London and back across France – took place during a crucial period with mounting religious tensions, dynastic rivalries, and war. Leaving Italy, the caravan travelled across Bavaria, Franconia, Baden Wurttemberg, and Rhineland Palatinate, stopping in cities and at courts, and meeting with networks of Italian merchants, Jesuits, bishops, diplomats, local rulers, and German nobles.

The first forty-nine watercolour drawings in Pomarancio's costume album offer an exclusively male representation of the German imperial political, military, and social hierarchies, partly along the lines of Renaissance iconographic conventions, starting with the emperor 'of the Romans', secular and religious electors, nobles, and city burghers, all with their coat of arms. Each page includes a figure set inside a simple frame with a caption in Italian; what is unique is how Pomarancio used the German princes to demonstrate regional fashions. Did his watercolour drawings portray some of the men the travellers met in the imperial lands? They do not match any of the circulating images on Germany in costume books, such as those by Weigel, Vecellio, De Bruyn, and

Boissard. In sharp contrast to the latter, which represent women, workers, and peasants, Pomarancio's sketches offer an unusual and original view of male political power. Therefore, the drawings very likely mirror portraits from life and are connected to the experience of travelling with his patron across German lands.

Quite surprisingly, the second part of the album displays fifty-seven male and female costumes figuring the political, social, and religious hierarchies of the Ottoman Empire. Pomarancio had never travelled there, and the five-month grand tour did not include the Balkan regions, the eastern Mediterranean, or Istanbul. Indeed, these drawings and their captions are entirely copied from the second edition – printed in Venice (1580) – of Nicolas de Nicolay's (1517–83) bestselling *Les Quatre premiers livres de Navigations et Peregrinations*. Printed in Lyon in 1567–8, it includes text and images by the French geographer who travelled to Istanbul on a diplomatic mission in 1551. Nicolay's subject position as a first-hand observer and direct witness of what he described and portrayed explains the extraordinary success of *Navigations*, which offered one of the earliest and most accurate depictions of the Ottoman world to be published in Europe, with sixty engravings by Louis Danet, based on Nicolay's original drawings (Brafman, 2009: 153–60). The book was reissued and translated in Italian, Dutch, English, and German (Mukerji, 2013: 151–69). It had a long-lasting influence on European costume books and albums, shaping Western views of the Levant up to the nineteenth century.[7] Within this important European circulation of images in albums and books, Pomarancio's drawings introduce us to an authored and dated manuscript for which we know the context of production and the dedicatee. This rare opportunity allows us to ask a very precise question: why did Vincenzo Giustiniani ask Pomarancio to make him a copy of the 1580 Venetian edition of Nicolay's book, the most complete edition? This edition, translated into Italian, added seven previously unpublished illustrations and displayed some of the first information on ethnic costumes of men and women in the Ottoman Empire.

[7] Francois Desprez, in *Recueil de la diversité des habits* (1567), reproduced two similar engravings, and Abraham de Bruyn, in *Omnium pene Europae, Asiae, Aphricae atque Americae gentium habitus* (1581), traced all of Nicolay's engravings. In Italy, Pietro Bertelli and Cesare Vecellio borrowed extensively from Nicolay. The prints in *Navigations* appeared in private costume albums, as in the anonymous one (1587) stored today in the L. A. Mayer Library in Jerusalem and in the beautifully coloured album *Théatre de tous le peuples et nations de la terre, avec leurs habits et ornéments divers tant anciens que modernes* by the Flemish painter Lucas de Heere (1534–84).

Chios, a Genoese Colony

To answer these questions, we must take a step back into Vincenzo Giustiniani's 'somewhat marginal position in Roman society', and into the origins of the Giustiniani family and fortune in the Genoese colonies of the eastern Mediterranean (Haskell, 1980: 95). This takes us to the Aegean island of Chios, in the Greek archipelago, then under Ottoman rule, where the Giustinianis ruled for two centuries. Vincenzo was born in Chios, where different Giustiniani branches, beginning in 1362, united in a business partnership – a *maona* – for the production, export, and sale of mastic throughout the Mediterranean and Asia, in a regime of monopoly and of rigid regulation of the local Greek workforce (agricultural labourers were sentenced to death if they were caught harvesting mastic beyond the *maona*'s control). Chios under the Giustinianis' rule was also a safe harbour for fugitive Christian prisoners and slaves.

In 1566, when Vincenzo was only two years old, the Turks took over the island, sacked and massacred the population, and turned the churches into mosques. One of the most tragic events recorded was the capture of eighteen Giustiniani children, who were taken to Istanbul and, refusing to convert to Islam, tortured and put to death.[8] The Giustinianis dispersed across the Mediterranean. Vincenzo managed to reach his father, Giuseppe, and older brother, Benedetto, in Rome, where the family took refuge owing to the protection of a maternal uncle who was a cardinal. In a few years, Giuseppe Giustiniani became one of the wealthiest bankers in Rome, and Benedetto was named cardinal.

Fifteen years before these tragic events – on 10 September 1551 – Nicolas de Nicolay arrived in Chios with the retinue of the French ambassador Gabriel d'Aramon. Due to a gathering storm, the convoy could not sail immediately to Istanbul and remained on the island for a few days. This allowed Nicolay to observe, describe, and talk to the local inhabitants of different ethnic groups – Greek, Genoese, and a large community of Jews. Nicolay provided a long and detailed description of the island's landscape and of the city of Chios, its buildings, churches, streets, and harbour. Young and married women wearing velvet, damask, and silk were 'so naturally attractive both in looks, manner and conversation that they are more like nymphs and goddesses than mortals' (Nicolay, 1580: 38). He also included two prints of women from Chios, drawn from real life – the young woman and the married one (Figures 14 and 15) – which Pomarancio copied (Figures 16 and 17).

---

[8] The memory of the Giustiniani massacre lingered in the public memory, and, in 1713, the Neapolitan painter Francesco Solimena (1657–1747) prepared three large sketches of the 'Massacro dei Giustiniani a Scio' for the frescoes decorating the Sala del Minor Consiglio in Genoa – destroyed in a fire in 1777.

Figure 14 Nicolas de Nicolay, *Navigazioni e viaggi* (1580) *Young woman from Chios*. Printed with the permission of the Ministero dei Beni Culturali/ Biblioteca Nazionale Centrale, Firenze. No additional reproductions of this image are permitted.

In his book, Nicolay dwells on the seasonal production of mastic from mastic trees in the hands of local agricultural labourers under the supervision of four Signori Giustiniani, each with his staff responsible for exporting mastic to one of four different markets: Greece; Italy, Spain, France, and Germany; Turkey; and Syria, Egypt, and North Africa. He talks to the locals and gives entertaining information on plants and animals. He discusses the political government of the republic, which belongs to the 'Maona which assembles the first gentlemen of the noble house of the Giustiniani of the Genoese nation' (Nicolay, 1580: 37).

Figure 15 Nicolas de Nicolay, *Navigazioni e viaggi* (1580) *Woman from the island of Chios* Printed with the permission of the Ministero dei Beni Culturali/ Biblioteca Nazionale Centrale, Firenze. No additional reproductions of this image are permitted.

During the few days spent on the island, Nicolay met Giuseppe Giustiniani, father of Vincenzo and consul of France, Venice, and Ragusa, who brought gifts to the French ambassador and greeted the guests.

The French geographer visited Chios when Vincenzo Giustiniani was still living on the island ruled by his family, fifteen years before its seizure in 1566, and *Navigations* was printed one year after its fall.[9] This first-hand account of

[9] The French naturalist Pierre Belon also visited Chios when it was still a Genoese colony. His *Observations de plusieurs singularités & choses mémorables, trouvées en Grèce, Asie, Judée,*

Figure 16 Pomarancio, *Disegni di figura*, *Young woman from the island of Chios*. Courtesy of the Gabinetto dei Disegni e delle Stampe, Galleria degli Uffizi, Florence

Chios before it was conquered by the Ottomans describes the land as a sort of earthly paradise from which the Giustiniani family came and where Vincenzo was born. The feeling of belonging to both the Aegean island and Genoa was part of what Haskell defined as Vincenzo's 'somewhat marginal position in Roman society', his being perceived as a foreigner. In his palace in Bassano di Sutri, renovated after he received the title of *marchese* from the pope in 1605, the large entrance hall is decorated with a fresco depicting the island of Chios and Genoa facing one another. Guests entering the palace were immediately reminded that their host was born in the Ottoman Empire in a colony of the Genoese republic (Strunck, 2003: 147–92).

Egypte, Arabie & autres pays étranges was printed in 1555. The description of Chios has no images.

Figure 17 Pomarancio, *Disegni di figura*, *Woman from the island of Chios*. Courtesy of the Gabinetto dei Disegni e delle Stampe, Galleria degli Uffizi, Florence

At the request of his patron, Pomarancio made a copy of Nicolay's illustrations for what probably was a personal album of memories. This adds a more intimate and emotional meaning to the wider European circulation of *Navigations* and to the extensive copying of the engravings in Northern European costume books and albums. It also adds Rome, with its artistic patronage and its new élites migrating into the city from the Christian diaspora across the Mediterranean, as a peculiar context enlarging the traditional view of Venice as the main Italian *porta d'Oriente*, where engravings of exotic costumes were mostly printed and circulated. For Vincenzo Giustiniani, Pomarancio's drawings after Nicolay's engravings probably revived memories of family traditions and perhaps nostalgia for a historical past prior to 1566, which still reverberated in the topography of the Bassano di Sutri frescoes.

The making of Pomarancio's album of costumes highlights some distinguishing features of this genre: it was a movable and flexible visual medium, partly picturing first- hand direct experience, partly reproducing images that circulated in a well-known printed book (Frazer, 2020). The agency of the patron was of crucial importance for the artist, who assembled the materiality and content, customizing it to the taste of the collector. Pomarancio juxtaposed his original drawings of German nobles in regional costumes to those traced from Nicolay's *Navigations* and created Vincenzo Giustiniani's unique album shaped by the experience of travel and the memory of migration. Moving from Pomarancio's reproduction of Nicolas de Nicolay's plates, the following pages expand into the vast European circulation of Nicolay's icons, paying special attention to the role of Christian minorities in the Ottoman Empire.

Contact Zones and Christian Minorities

Nicolay's work needs to be set within the dense intellectual, commercial, and political exchanges between the Ottoman world and Europe that prepared the production of the new geographies of the late fifteenth and early sixteenth centuries (Manners, 2007). Probably sent by the king of France, Charles IX, to study fortifications, Nicolay travelled to Constantinople between July 1551 and July 1552, and, after his return to France, he was named 'géographe ordinaire du Rois'. His figures became archetypes and were reproduced in at least eight costume books published before 1601 (Wilson, 2007: 110). They provided the basis for most of the Turkish costumes in Vecellio's *Degli habiti antichi e moderni* (1590), discussed in the following paragraphs. With its important European diffusion, *Navigations* originated an orientalizing process, which rapidly produced a selective aesthetic, a peculiar taste for certain images, clothes, and gestures that spread and consolidated a Western European imagery of the multi-ethnic and multireligious structure of the Ottoman Empire (Guérin Dalle Mese, 1998: 53–115; Wilson, 2007).

A handful of plates picturing Christian minorities in the Ottoman Empire – the slave élite of men and women from non-Muslim backgrounds, trained in the military corps of the Janissaries and inside the harem as concubines – were particularly meaningful for Venetian artists (Peirce, 1993; Pedani, 2010; Masters, 2016). Nicolay relied on two contemporary authors claiming a direct experience of the inner workings of the Ottoman court owing to their upbringing as Christian slaves in the Serail. He copied text from these two Venetians, Giuseppe Bassano and Antonio Menavino (Bassano, 1545; Menavino, 1548), both of whom had been kidnapped and enslaved. Nicolay was assisted by a eunuch from Ragusa, Zaferaga, who had been trained since his early youth in the Serail. 'As soon as he understood my desire to draw the costumes of the women, Zaferaga had two Turkish prostitutes (*femmes publiques*) dress up for me with very rich clothes that he sent for from the market, the *bezestan*, where

Figure 18 Nicolas de Nicolay, *Navigazioni e viaggi* (1580) *Turkish Lady at home, i.e. in the Serail.* Printed with the permission of the Ministero dei Beni Culturali/Biblioteca Nazionale Centrale, Firenze. No additional reproductions of this image are permitted.

one can buy any kind of attire. They are the women I portrayed in the following drawings' (Nicolay, 1989: 129). Figures 18 and 19 portray such women.

The gaze of the Ragousan eunuch, his choice of women, and ornaments are therefore a constitutive feature of Nicolay's perception and representation of the female slave élite in the sultan's harem. Its inaccessibility produced a staging of identities where camouflage and mimicry are the main components of the visual experience. Nicolay's attention, shaped by Zaferaga's interpretation and cultural mediation, focussed on appearances, language, and religion. The plates had wide circulation with their two prints of the *azamoglans*, the Christian male

Figure 19 Cesare Vecellio, *Habiti* (1598) *Turkish woman*. Berenson Library, Villa I Tatti

children sent as a tribute to the Sublime Porte – that is, the central government – from the peasant households of the continental European parts of the empire, mainly the Balkans (Figure 20).

Nicolay entertained readers with anecdotes that enriched his plates with first-hand accounts. In Adrianople, when accompanying Ambassador d'Aramon to the house of the local pasha, the first *visir* of the empire, Nicolay saw a *delly* – a blustering warrior scorning wounds and death as an unpaid irregular troop of Serbian origin in the Turkish army (Figure 21). Offering the *delly* some money, Nicolay invited him to the ambassador's lodgings, where he drew the *delly's* portrait featuring his strange costume. A few days later, as the army was moving

Figure 20 Nicolas de Nicolay, *Navigazioni e viaggi* (1580) *Azamoglan*. Printed with the permission of the Ministero dei Beni Culturali/Biblioteca Nazionale Centrale, Firenze. No additional reproductions of this image are permitted.

to Transylvania, Nicolay saw the *delly* riding a handsome Turkish horse that was 'envelopped in the whole skin of a huge lion whose front paws were attached to the horse's neck and the other were hanging on the back' (Nicolay, 1989: 227). Turning to an interpreter, Nicolay asked the *delly* about his religion and origin: the *delly* answered he came from Serbia and was born a Christian but dissimulated his faith behind Islamic practice. He then pronounced in Greek and in 'sclavonic' language the Christian Sunday prayers. When asked why he dressed so strangely with huge wings, he said it was to

Figure 21 Nicolas de Nicolay, *Navigazioni e viaggi 1580, Delly*. Printed with the permission of the Ministero dei Beni Culturali/Biblioteca Nazionale Centrale, Firenze. No additional reproductions of this image are permitted.

appear more furious and terrifying when facing the enemy (Nicolay, 1989: 227).[10] The *delly* became iconic in European costume books.

Gentlewomen and Dalmatine in Venetian Outposts and Territories

Christian minorities mainly came from the European lands of the Ottoman Empire. The following pages focus on the Balkans, a geopolitical region

[10] Melchior Lorck, the Danish-German artist who served as a member of the imperial embassy between 1555 and 1559 under the leadership of Ambassador Ogier Ghislain de Busbecq, made a fine engraving of the *delly* (Fischer, 2009; Busbecq, 2010).

under-researched in most studies of early modern Europe. These sections of Nicolay's work (books III and IV) were particularly important for Venetian artists, given that some of the Balkan territories were part of the Venetian overseas colonies where the Ottoman and European worlds overlapped. For a more nuanced understanding of these contact zones, avoiding the traditional clear-cut opposition between East and West, we can focus on the fluid identities of Christians moving across languages and religions on the frontiers between the Ottoman Empire, the Venetian Stato da Mar, and the Habsburg Empire (Todorova, 1997; Greene, 2000; Woolf, 2002; Rothman, 2012a).

Tracing the representation of costumes and customs from the Balkan peninsula in sixteenth-century Europe requires a constant crossing of borders between the contested and changing territories of three empires of different dimensions. Though Venice lost a considerable number of territories to the Ottomans, most notably Cyprus in 1571, it retained control of the overseas lands comprising Dalmatia, the Adriatic and Ionian islands, Morea (the Peloponnesus), and Candia (Crete). Durazzo and Split became the main commercial ports of the eastern trade. The Habsburg Empire controlled the northern part of the area, which included the southern Austrian regions of Carinthia, Carniola, and Trieste, as well as the kingdom of Hungary, comprising a part of Croatia and Zagreb. The Balkan peninsula, largely under Ottoman rule, was the route from Venice to Istanbul, which, from the Asian side, brought silk and spices to Venice, along with immigrants from Croatia, Dalmatia, Slovenia, Turkey, and the Ottoman Empire.

The clothed bodies of men and women from these regions appear in scattered images situated within the Hungarian kingdom, the Ottoman and Habsburg Empires, the independent city of Ragusa (now Dubrovnik) and the Venetian overseas colonies. A transcultural and trans-regional approach implies crossing religious and ethnic borders in constant tension in the age of the Counter-Reformation: Latin and Orthodox Christianity, Islam, and Judaism. Captives, fugitives, slaves, and converts were part of broad networks of communication, information, exchange, and trade across the Mediterranean. Representing Balkan dress therefore means locating ethnic, linguistic, and religious communities inside large-scale competing political entities where bodies and attire were often sites of camouflaged and ambivalent identities and where minorities marked their traditions mostly through ritual and the costumes of women (Born, 2011; Calvi, 2011).

In Italy, there probably was no other printed image of Balkan clothing before Vecellio's *Degli habiti antichi e moderni* (1590).[11] The Venetian artist broke the

[11] Earlier costume books copied Nicolay's prints. A few were published in 1568 by Ferdinando Bertelli portraying Hungarians and 'Sclavonians'.The first drawings of the costumes of the inhabitants of Ragusa are in Pietro Bertelli's *Diversarum Nationum Habitus* (Padua, 1589). In Northern Europe, the Flemish engraver De Bruyn, in the first edition of his *Omnium pene*

unchallenged visual monopoly surrounding Nicolay's images. This decision was especially significant in view of the artist's subject position that situated his gaze within the interests of the Venetian overseas colonies. Vecellio distributed his illustrations of Balkan costumes differently in the two editions of *Habiti antichi e moderni*. In the first, he included eight images of Hungarian, Croatian, and Dalmatian clothing in the broad region of Helvetia, which comprised also Prussia, the Low Countries, Poland, and Russia. In the 1598 edition, he grouped them in book IX under the title *Habiti d'Ungheria* [*Hungarian Clothing*] and added the prince of Transylvania. Book IX thus displays nine plates – six male and three female figures. *Habiti d'Ungheria* belongs to territories not defined in terms of a distinct geographic and cultural unit, but rather as a fragmented set of lands divided between different political and religious systems, including both Christian and Islamic lands. Contemporary maps printed in Venice, namely those by the official geographer of the republic, Giacomo Gastaldi, represented the area along the same coordinates. In line with the prevailing intellectual trend in sixteenth-century Venetian political and historical writings (Valensi, 1987, 1990), Vecellio's text does not draw a line which separates Catholicism from Orthodox Christianity and Islam but insists on including these religious groups within Europe and the colonial interests of Venice. Compared to other costume books of the same period, such as those by Boissard, De Bruyn, and Bertelli, where images from this area are scattered in a haphazard way or set within Turkish, Armenian, Caramanic, and Greek costumes, Vecellio constructs a coherent set of tables and texts on the Balkans. In 1598, he adds the prince of Transylvania (presumably Sigismund Batory) in Western European armour. Introducing a clear hierarchical structure meant adjusting the Balkans to Europe and the world, as religious and secular rulers (the doge, the pope, the emperor, and all European and non-Western kings and princes) inaugurate Vecellio's representation of the peoples of the four known parts of the world.

Colour is a distinguishing feature of these costumes in all social milieux. In contrast to the prevailing black fashion spreading from Spain throughout Western Europe, Croats and Hungarians dress in colourful patterns with a taste for red (Figure 22). 'Hungarian men wear long garments especially in red. All of them wear buttons fastened with braided trim, some of silk mixed with gold and some of crystal' (Vecellio, 1598: 410; Rosenthal and Jones, 2008: 245). They are warlike people and that's why they wear high arched shoes with

---

Europae, Asiae, Aphricae, Americae gentium habitus (Antwerp, 1581), had already reproduced two images from Nicolay's *Livres* – the *Tabellarius ragusanus* and *Mercator ragusanus* – that, with the Macedonian woman, became iconic throughout Europe. In France, Jean Jacques Boissard, in his *Habitus Variarum Orbis Gentium* (Paris, 1581), pictured an Albanian, a man from Ragusa, and the woman from Macedonia

Figure 22 Cesare Vecellio, *Habiti* (1598) *Man from Croatia*. Berenson Library, Villa I Tatti

soles of iron. The emphasis on natural warlike attitudes will be endlessly repeated in travel journals up to the nineteenth century. A loose society of aggressive men, which in the eighteenth century will be increasingly connected to the lack of civilization (Woolf, 2002), is gradually essentialized in Vecellio's text through a set of predominantly male portraits. They are Catholic and pious, bearing arms and hard-working.

Vecellio's gaze and point of view is that of a Venetian describing and drawing costumes that are part of the Stato da Mar. These are the lands that bred soldiers for the army and the navy of the republic, and the approach is biased by the rationale of colonial discourse: Dalmatians in the service of Venice are devout

Figure 23 Cesare Vecellio, *Habiti* (1598) *Gentlewomen in Venetian outposts*. Berenson Library, Villa I Tatti

Christians fighting for the true faith in the Mediterranean. Venetian rule over Dalmatia is pictured in the costumes of 'Gentlewomen in Venetian outposts and Territories', as well as in the simpler garb of the Dalmatine (Figures 23, 24, and 25). Local and Venetian women of the élite embody networks of alliance, hierarchy, and ethnicity. Dress appears first and foremost as a cultural technology of rule within what Bernard Cohn defines as a 'theatre for state experimentation' (Cohn, 1996: XI).

The magnificence of dress is a gendered function of title and rank, and the Venetian women of the ruling élite are the arbiters of fashion.

Figure 24 Cesare Vecellio, *Habiti* (1598) *Man from Dalmatia*. Berenson Library, Villa I Tatti

> The wives of gentlemen sent to govern other cities take on their husbands titles and are called *Podestaresse*, *Capitane* and so on. Certain elegant fashions are also named after these unusual titles, following decorum. For this reason, these women dress very magnificently and wear many ornaments. Their gowns are of different colours of brocade, silk, gold, and silver. They dress their hair always blonde (by nature or by art), very richly with pearls and other jewels. (Rosenthal and Jones, 2008: 135)

The sumptuous clothes of the *podestaresse* and *capitane* as well as those of the local gentlewomen imitating Venetian fashion transgress the sumptuary laws of the metropole and are an essential element in the constitution of

Figure 25 Cesare Vecellio, *Habiti* (1598) *Woman from Dalmatia*. Berenson Library, Villa I Tatti

authority. As Cohn forcefully observes, clothes cannot be understood only as metaphors of power and authority. In many contexts, 'authority is literally part of the body of those who possess it' (Cohn, 1996: 114). Venetian women in Dalmatia embody a powerful identification between dress and colonial rule.

In striking contrast to the stiff bodies and precious dresses of the ruling élite, Vecellio pictures the local woman from Dalmatia in her colourful, simple, and loose clothing (she wears no bodice). The 'tall healthy and active' Dalmatina looks very graceful in her *ghellero*, a short 'open and roomy garment of fine wool or satin or damasco with half-length sleeves' (Rosenthal and Jones, 2008: 347).

Figure 26 Cesare Vecellio, *Habiti* (1598) *Young woman from Ragusa*. Berenson Library, Villa I Tatti

Like their men, these women are very pious. Those living on the island of Cres come to Venice every year for the feast of the Ascension, wearing head veils of thin silk, long coloured woollen gowns, linen aprons, and thin *camicie* without ruffles (Vecellio, 1598: 412–13; Rosenthal and Jones, 2008: 347–8).

The last table of Vecellio's book IX pictures the young woman of the republic of Ragusa (now Dubrovnik) (Figure 26). She is a bride of the local nobility, wearing the Venetian-styled black mantle *buratto* (Vecellio, 1598: 415; Rosenthal and Jones, 2008: 350).

Picturing the young woman of Ragusa in a black cloak emphasized Venetian influence, visible in the fashions adopted by the local patriciate and citizenry that had close ties to the Venetian republic (Krekic, 1997; Bertelli, 2004). The *giovanetta ragusea* expressed the point of view of the Venetian artist, which was not neutral. He portrayed southern Slavs who kept a Christian identity even when subject to the Ottomans and were connected to Venice through war, migration, or social and political networks within a semi-colonial or colonial relationship to the power of the *Dominante* (Arbel, 1996, 2013; Todorova, 1997). They liked to dress in a colourful way. The women disliked black and bodices. The men wore golden and crystal buttons and small hats lined with fur, and often carried scimitars and daggers. Their style and choice of garments was common to many of the Slavs stretching from Dalmatia, Croatia, and Bosnia to Poland and Russia. Vecellio chose to include them in a separate book where he did not reproduce Nicolay's engravings, but probably drew his models from direct visual experience (Newton, 1988).

Ottoman Costume Albums

Analytic perspectives that focus on circulation and connection, rather than influence and imitation, are crucial in bringing to light processes of cultural translation across the Mediterranean (Gerritsen and Riello, 2015; Gurkan, 2015; Frazer, 2020a). Recent research has emphasized the collaborative dimension of such cultural exchanges that concentrate on diplomacy as a 'trans-imperial' contact zone for the production and communication of information and knowledge (Rothman 2009, 2012a, 2021; Um and Clarke, 2016). The following pages address the contacts and exchanges between Western diplomats, travellers, and European and Ottoman artists, all of whom helped to shape the making and collecting of Ottoman costume albums. The analytical emphasis is once more on the flexible and mobile configuration of the albums, their often anonymous origin, the agency of artists and patrons, and their displacement across long-distance networks.

In Istanbul, Nicolas de Nicolay and Melchior Lorck worked in the diplomatic milieu of the Sublime Porte. Ambassadors travelled with their own artists, who spent a few years in the Ottoman Empire, drawing, engraving, travelling, and portraying high officials and members of the court, women in and out of the harem, rituals, processions, punishments, and festivities. The diplomatic milieu was a crucial filter mediating and constructing textual and visual information for the European public, particularly through Western costume and portrait books (Wilson, 2007: 101).

Figure 27 Taeschner Album. *The Venetian bailo's house* (Wikimedia Commons)

Diplomats and Travellers

Venetian ambassadors, *baili*, and European diplomats also collected costume albums drawn by Ottoman artists, which are now in many libraries in Europe. One of them is the Taeschner album, in the collection of the German orientalist Franz Taeschner, who first published it in 1924 (Alt-Stambuler Hof-Und Volksleben, 1925).[12] This seventeenth-century Turkish miniature album of European origin measures 30 x 20 cm; on the front side of the fifty-five folios, a miniature is pasted on each page, probably by a Turkish hand (Figure 27). Taeschner translated into German the original Italian captions and argued that the album was produced in the Venetian diplomatic milieu owing to the style of some images and costumes, picturing the residence and garden of the Venetian *bailo*, a carnival street parade and the Venetian cannoning of Tenedos, among the portrait of Sultan Ahmed I and the high-ranking officials and staff of his palace.

Taeschner believed that the themes of the images corresponded to the interests of the Europeans coming to Turkey, and he therefore thought that they were done by a Turk and commissioned by a European, such as the Venetian *bailo* of the time, who may have been the first owner of the album. These manuscript

[12] The album was exposed in the year 1910 at the Munich Exhibition of Muslim Art. The original album is lost.

collections of costumes were often attached to travel or diplomatic reports from Turkey and pictured interesting details of oriental life (Taeschner, 1925, *Vorbemerkung*).

The Taeschner album shows important stylistic similarities with the Cicogna Codex, dating to the early 1660s and now housed in the Museo Civico Correr in Venice, which Natalie Rothman has recently studied. The Codex highlights the role of Italian, especially Venetian *dragomans* (diplomatic interpreters) in mediating objects and texts and in translating practices across Ottoman and European spaces. The manuscript was probably 'assembled in the house of the Venetian *bailo* in Istanbul through collaboration between a Venetian diplomat and his dragomans, Ottoman miniaturists, and Italian draftsmen as a guidebook to Ottoman society' (Rothman, 2012b: 43). The production of such albums, whether by local artists connected to the court or active in the bazaar milieu in Istanbul, or by European artists, points to a continuing cooperation between Ottomans and Europeans. Situated in the context of Mediterranean diplomacy, the Taeschner and Cicogna Codex were probably part of the same manuscript (Rothman, 2012b: 62).

Venice was a repository for such albums, initially produced by Western artists in Istanbul in the European tradition of costume books and, beginning in the seventeenth century, by Ottoman artists who appropriated these models, re-signifying them through local traditions that pictured in a stylized manner a rather fixed set of images featuring the sultan, the imperial court, and the city. In contrast to the global breadth of costume books such as Vecellio's *Habiti*, albums produced in Istanbul repeated similar icon setting on stage, in a sort of paper theatre, the court, and the city. They portrayed the military and religious hierarchies as well as the urban trades and types: women going to the bath, janissaries, the eunuch, the sultana, the butcher, the cook, the street barber (Wilson, 2007). As the following paragraphs show, these collections of clothing commissioned by diplomats, scholars, and travellers were understood as guidebooks to the city and portable cabinets of curiosities.

From the early seventeenth century onwards, costume albums appealed to a widening urban market of collectors and travellers, beyond diplomatic circles. Describing his stay in Istanbul, Peter Mundy wrote in his *Book of Travels*, 'For the several habits used att Constantinople, where most officers and Nationes are distinguished by their habits, I have a little booke ... painted by the Turks themselves in Anno 1618, although no great art therein, yet enough to satisfie concerning that Matter.' Decorative paper cuttings embellish the pages where Mundy often wrote his lengthy comments (Mundy, 1907: 26–7; Collaco, 2017: 257–8; Kynan-Wilson, 2017) (Figure 28).

Europeans collected costume albums in Istanbul, not only for personal use and entertainment, but also for the enjoyment of curious people back at home (Cardini,

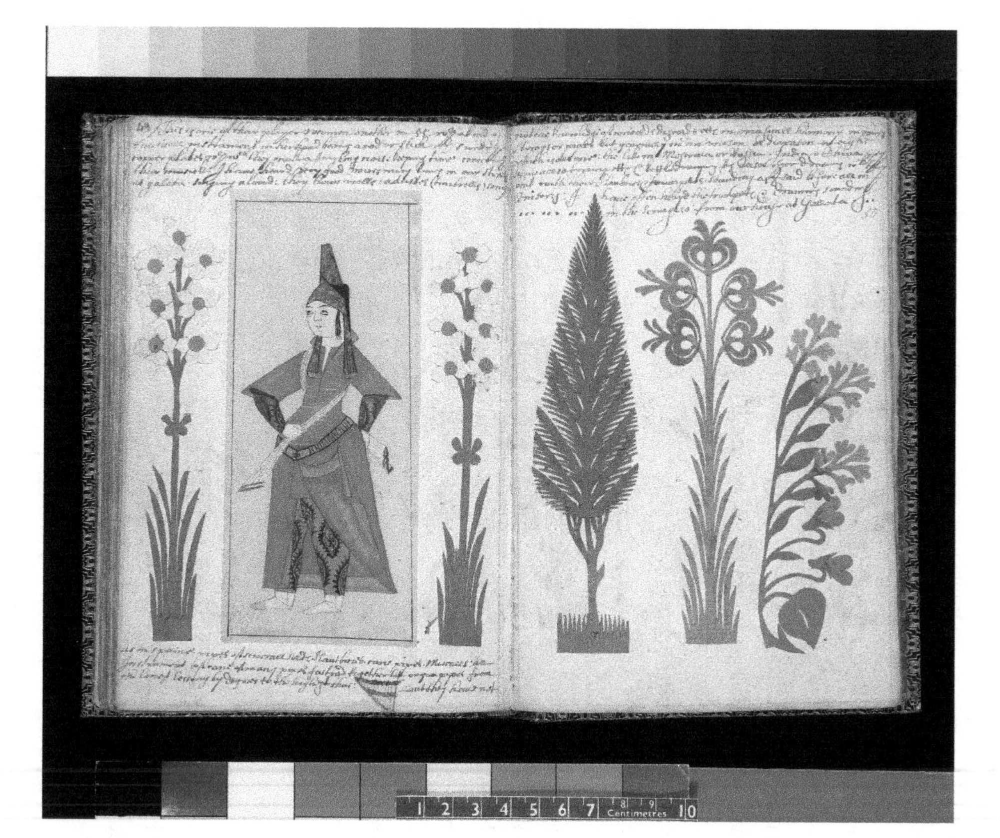

Figure 28 Peter Mundy, *Young woman of rank*, in *A briefe relation of the Turckes, their kings, Emperors or Grandsigneurs, their conquest, religion, customes, habits etc*. Istanbul 1618 (The Trustees of the British Museum)

2001: 248). The Italian merchant Pietro della Valle in a letter from Constantinople (1614) mentions that he has commissioned more than sixty images of 'coloured figures ... in which all the diverse clothes of every sort, both of the men and women of this city will be drawn from life' for a friend back in Italy (Della Valle, 1989: 14). He will bind them in a book and write two- or three-line captions under each figure. Mundy's and Della Valle's albums highlight the curator's agency in the choice and outlay of the pages. This was a crucial feature of the costume album as was the selection of images: whether such drawings were to be considered 'art', as Mundy suggests, was another matter. As we shall see in the following pages, European collectors and publishers, especially in the eighteenth and nineteenth centuries, altered and embellished images by non-Western painters, considering them primitive and technically unskilled.

The widespread repetition of genres, scenes, and figures in manuscript collections of clothing has led scholars to suggest a mass production in Istanbul, in ateliers specializing in such miniatures for a broad clientele for whom they provided a stock of characters that could be inscribed, framed, and personalized to suit individual buyers. Further examples of the proliferation of the same technique and models appear as late as the 1650s in the album collected by Claes Rålamb, the Swedish ambassador to Istanbul (Collaço, 2017: 261).

The Rålamb Book of Costumes

The *Rålambska dräktboken* (*The Rålamb Book of Costumes*) was purchased by Claes Rålamb (1622–98) in Constantinople in 1657–8, where King Charles X Gustaf of Sweden sent him as an envoy to Sultan Mehmed IV's court. It was the first Swedish embassy to the Sublime Porte and, while in Istanbul, Rålamb commissioned twenty large paintings in oil on canvas, depicting a remarkably detailed imperial procession that took place in September 1657. It included the sultan, the grand vizier, and high-ranking officers and courtiers, and it ended with cooks, gardeners, and water carriers painted in a stylized manner by a local unidentified artist who probably used a set of pre-existing stereotyped models. Indeed, the costumes and uniforms of the men correspond closely to some of the images of the small costume book that the Swedish diplomat acquired in Istanbul and is now in the Nordic Library in Stockholm (Adahl, 2006: 35). It is a *muraqqa*, a type of picture album popular among collectors and usually put together from several different sources. (Kondak, 2009). The *muraqqa* closely resembles the German *Stammbuch* and the *album amicorum*, where travellers and students in Europe gathered coats of arms, portraits, genre scenes, images copied from costume books, small texts, and signatures from friends and mentors (Wilson, 2005: 104–20; Rosenthal, 2007; Rublack, 2010: 221–9).

Figure 29 *Rålamb album. An egg seller.* Courtesy of the National Library of Sweden.

Rålamb's album contains 121 colorful miniature drawings of Turkish officials, people of various trades, different ethnic groups, and women (Figures 29–34). The drawings are in India ink with gouache and some gilding. Most of the folios have notes in Swedish, French, Italian, or Latin describing the miniature in question as well as notes made by Rålamb himself. Recent scholarship has suggested that the images by an anonymous artist in Istanbul were completed by a Polish painter and, after the diplomat's return home, by an anonymous local artist in Sweden (Adahl, 2006: 39). Western stylistic techniques such as realism and depth were embedded in the Ottoman miniature drawings of the album, which includes a wider variety of ethnic types (Armenians, Jews, Greeks), professions (women musicians), and trades than the Taeschner and Cicogna manuscript collections of clothing. The following images illustrate this variety. Folios of different sizes are bound together and display on each front a single water-coloured, dressed figure on an empty background with multilingual captions set in a simple frame, in the tradition of European costume books. The images communicate a keen attention to gestures, details, and accessories.

Figure 30 *Rålamb album. A woman musician.* Courtesy of the National Library of Sweden.

Because of the asymmetric binding and the different sizes of the folios, each figure shows details (heads, legs, feet) of the following image. The cumulative process which underscores the album is thus visible suggesting a personal selection of characters probably chosen by Rålamb himself.

Frederick Stibbert's Costume Collection

A further to-date-unexplored northern circulation of some thirty images, traced from the Taeschner, Cicogna, and Rålamb albums, is today in Florence, in the Library of Frederick Stibbert, originally collected and arranged at the end of the eighteenth century by Richard Bull, an English landowner, politician, and keen collector of prints, drawings, and books on the Isle of Wight.[13] This extraordinary collection brings together, in colour, 2,922 prints and 631 drawings of ancient and modern costumes from all parts of the

[13] *A Series of Prints and Drawings Serving to Illustrate the Modes and Fashions of Ancient and Modern Dresses in Different Parts of the World, 1792*, vol. 1. The plates were inlaid by Staggemier. The collection of costumes is displayed in seven red morocco-bound, large-folio volumes.

Figure 31 *Rålamb album. A carrier of food for the Serail*. Courtesy of the National Library of Sweden.

Figure 32 *Rålamb album. Armenian woman*. Courtesy of the National Library of Sweden.

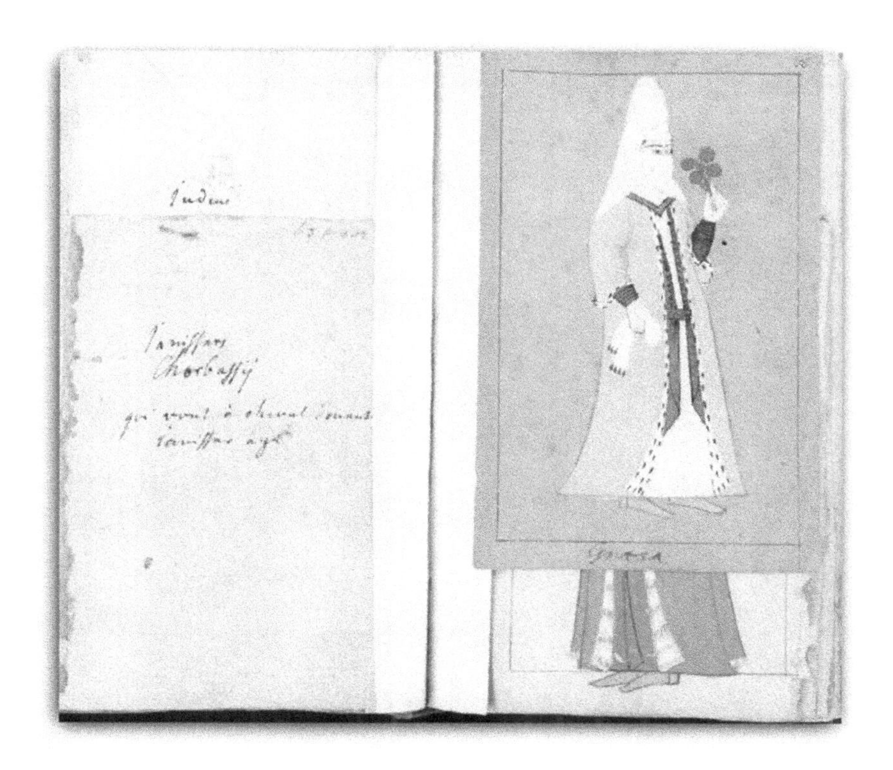

Figure 33 *Rålamb album. A Greek woman*. Courtesy of the National Library of Sweden.

Figure 34 *Rålamb album. A Citizen of Constantinople*. Courtesy of the National Library of Sweden.

Figure 35 Florence. Stibbert Library. *A Series of Prints and Drawings*, vol. 1, *Turkish Costumes. Street vendors and trades*

world (Figure 35). The six images on the same folio display a set of hand-coloured vendors and trades: (from upper left corner) a carrier of wood; a woman and child taking merchandise to the market; a man with a dog carrying a spit; a broom seller; a water carrier. Richard Bull proceeded to Westernize

Figure 36 Stibbert Library, *A bride*

the images, which were embellished with vivid watercolours and enhanced in gold, displayed in groups of six on each folio, and listed in a table of contents. Grouping the images thematically altered the narrative sequence of the albums that pictured individual figures on a single sheet. Furthermore, the table of contents introduced a scholarly angle to the collection that inevitably Europeanized its internal organization.

The Turkish costumes from the seventeenth and eighteenth centuries display hand-coloured images of the military and religious hierarchies, of minor court personnel, women musicians, street vendors, and workers. They have captions in Turkish, Arabic, and French, pointing to a non-Italian audience. Four prints portray different types of punishments and tortures with gruesome details repeating those in the Taeschner album and Cicogna Codex.

Figures 36–49 show visual analogies between the Stibbert, Rålamb, and Taeschner albums.

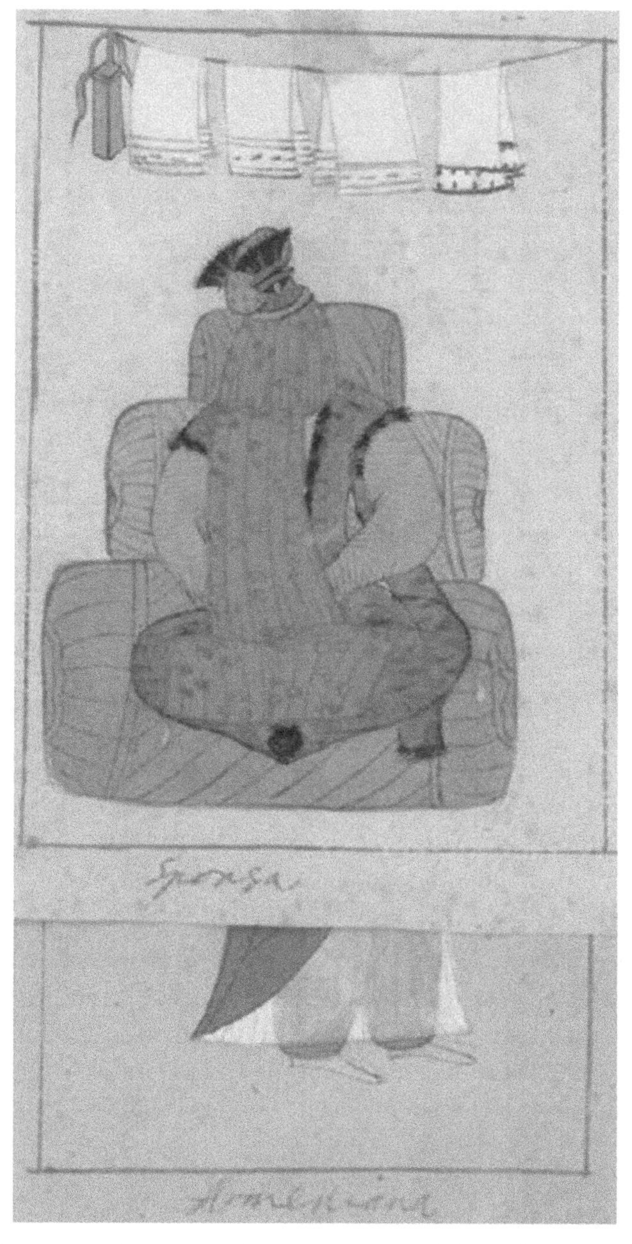

Figure 37 Rålamb album, *A bride*. Courtesy of the National Library of Sweden

These thirteen images lend themselves to a comparative analysis. Types, functions, and trades display ethnicity, gender, and status connected to court and social hierarchies. The Stibbert collection of Turkish costumes exhibits

Figure 38 Stibbert Library, *A Turkish woman*

more vivid colours and some golden heightening. Similar images (Figures 44, 45, 48, and 49) show different colours and slightly dissimilar gestures. Some characters are presented from a left or a right angle and some figures have more depth (Figures 42 and 43). They probably came from a pre-existing stock of images from which buyers could choose.

Istanbul, Venice, Munster, Stockholm, the Isle of Wight, Florence: to what extent did this circulation and copying of images alter their meaning? The layout and display of the icons in the pages of the nineteenth-century morocco-bound volume in the Stibbert Library selected and embellished a few exotic-looking characters and scenes that appealed to the well-trained orientalizing gaze of a collector in the age of Britain's imperial domination. A comparative reading of the albums highlights common features: captions in different languages that reflect changing ownership and readers disseminated,

Figure 39 Rålamb album, *A Turkish woman*. Courtesy of the National Library of Sweden

as it were, across visual contact zones over a long time span. This circulation points to the popularity of the genre embedded in processes of cultural translation and reinterpretation.

The concluding section concentrates on the experimental format and the mobility of costume albums in the eighteenth century and on the expanding art market catering to a growing urban clientele beyond the Ottoman Empire.

Experimental and Hybrid Styles

Ottoman costume albums have been contextualized within an evolving time frame: Western and Ottoman artists produced the albums for a European clientele in Istanbul in the sixteenth and seventeenth centuries, while Ottoman upper-middle-class patrons in the eighteenth century bought albums from local Ottoman artists (Schick, 2004). Western figurative conventions appealing to European travellers and buyers joined with local visual culture in albums produced in Istanbul. Portraying their society through the taxonomy of dress

Figure 40 Stibbert Library, *Punishment for sellers cheating on weight*

and using Western models, in the seventeenth century, Ottoman artists delved into social types and trades travellers might meet in the streets and started selling their single sheets in the market, broadening their social spectrum beyond the court. Picking up on a combination of ethnography, curiosity and iconic figures, clothing and gestures, these albums became very popular not only among foreigners, but also beyond Istanbul. By the late eighteenth century, a mix of experimental scenes decorated with Persian miniatures, Western (often Italian) images, and elaborate Turkish bindings were circulating among new Ottoman urban élites who collected 'bazaar paintings alongside more valued forms of art like calligraphy, as well as specimens from foreign lands and the Ottoman past, giving albums a status akin to portable Kunstkammers' (Collaco, 2018: 3).

Recent Ottomanist scholarship has questioned the prevailing Eurocentric attribution of agency to Western patrons, artists, and clientele, in the selection

Figure 41 Rålamb album, *Punishment for dishonest tradesmen*. Courtesy of the National Library of Sweden

and layout of the images, in the captions and comments often found in the albums, even when employing local artists. Ottoman manuscripts display a broad range of styles and subject matter from Persianate calligraphic specimens to figure studies inspired by European costume books. These complex visual interconnections shed light on a wide circulation of artistic production and on the collection of extravagantly illustrated albums in the Islamic world, among the Ottomans, Safavids, and Mughals from the sixteenth century to the nineteenth. Some albums contained European engravings, which may have started to feature in Islamic albums in the first half of the sixteenth century (Roxburgh, 2001). One of the albums contains Florentine prints datable to between 1460 and 1480; these seem to have been acquired during the reign of Mehmed II, when close political, mercantile, and cultural exchanges between Florence and the Ottomans were established. In the Safavid Empire, especially in the city of Isfahan, making albums was widely practised among the merchant and courtly classes of the time (Roxburgh, 2001: 7; Fetvaci, 2011: 243).

In a recent book, Emine Fetvaci analyses the structure and composition of the *Album of the World Emperor* made for Sultan Ahmed I (1603–17) by his

Figure 42 Stibbert Library, *Executioner carrying a severed head*

courtier Kalender Pasa (d. 1616). It has thirty-two folios containing an eclectic variety of styles and materials – painting, calligraphy, illumination – from different contexts, including portraits, depictions of entertainments, gatherings, and ethnic and social types from a variety of visual traditions – from Safavid Iran, Ottoman imitations of Persian miniatures, and Ottoman works similar to those produced in European costume books. This vast combination of models, medias, and styles, writes Fetvaci, 'points to the importance of viewing the artistic landscape of the early modern world as connected' (Fetvaci, 2019: 3). The mobility of prints, costume books, drawings, and calligraphic samples between Europe and the Islamic world and across imperial boundaries made the eclecticism of the *Album of the World Emperor* possible (Burke, 2016; Fetvaci, 2019). The trans-imperial networks that shape costume books and

Figure 43 Rålamb album, *Executioner carrying a severed head*. Courtesy of the National Library of Sweden

albums, as recent scholarly work insists, shed light, not only on Western perceptions, but also on the vogue for hybrid visual compilations among the rising urban élites in the Ottoman, Safavid, and Mughal Empires (Alfonso, 2016). The album with its experimental format underlines cross-cultural interaction and contacts among urban centres and new consumers keen to collect artworks. In addition to their popularity across the Ottoman, Safavid, and Mughal Empires, albums became popular in seventeenth-century China and – as Section 3 shows – in Japan.

Scholars are now questioning the parallel developments of a genre which, owing to its flexibility, encouraged the experimental compilations and far-reaching visual connections that shaped and in turn were shaped by a new consciousness of space and spatial relations (Campbell and Chong, 2005; Fetvacy, 2019: 5). Mostly originated in diplomatic trans-imperial networks, costume albums were characterized by cooperation among artists and patrons, flexibility of content, and circulation through travel, migration, and exchange across and beyond the Mediterranean. As a 'phenomenon', they are defined by their mutability (Raby, 2017). They were offered as gifts, collected, sold, and copied. Changing ownership altered the narrative sequence of the images and

Figure 44 Stibbert Library, *Executioner*

the materiality of the album bound and reworked in Europe – as in the case of Stibbert's Prints and Drawings collection. Multilingual captions were often added outlining the fundamental issue of cultural translation in multiethnic and multi-religious geopolitical contexts and across far-reaching networks of trade, collectionism, and diplomacy.

Figure 45 Rålamb album, *Executioner*. Courtesy of the National Library of Sweden

Figure 46 Stibbert Library, *A religious man playing the cymbals while praying*

Figure 47 Rålamb album, *A religious man*. Courtesy of the National Library of Sweden

Figure 48 Rålamb album, *A barber*. Courtesy of the National Library of Sweden

Figure 49 Taeschner album, *A barber.* Berenson Library, Villa I Tatti

3 Italy, Europe, and Japan

This section addresses visual and textual interconnections across the Pacific, focussing on agents, books, and diplomatic exchanges during the so-called Christian century in Japan (1549–1650) (Boxer, 1951). The crucial role of diplomatic exchanges and gifts and the role of Jesuit missionaries as negotiators of European knowledge and artistic production shape the making of costume books in Japan during the Edo period. As in the West, costume albums and books were part of a new visual culture of space, emerging with Renaissance geography, that displayed the representation of the people of the world on a variety of media: screens, maps, scrolls, books, and popular encyclopedias. A growing editorial production addressed an urban readership curious about the foreigners arriving in Japan and attracted to geographical and anthropological knowledge. Through the taxonomy of dress, the variety of the people of the world appeared in Japanese maps, screens, costume books, and scroll pictures. The images detail differences in bodily postures, skin colour, gestures, appearances, ornament, and accessories connecting to visual practices, which spread across Italy, Europe, and the Ottoman Empire. The greater status attributed to visual perception in the early modern period shaped the sartorial display and the hierarchy of appearances in Edo Japan.

In 1582, the first Japanese diplomatic mission arrived in Europe. It consisted of four Christianized samurai young men accompanied by Father Diogo de Mesquita of the Jesuits, who travelled to Western Europe across Portugal, Spain, and Italy (Brown, 1994; Cooper, 2005; Wilson, 2005; Boscaro, 2008). They visited Pope Gregory XIII in Rome and then moved up to Florence, Bologna, Venice, and beyond Genoa. The mission attracted crowds of onlookers and was accompanied by an important exchange of gifts. No Japanese had ever been seen before and European costume books had never included Japanese dress. This unique event encouraged Cesare Vecellio to update this visual tradition by drawing a young Japanese man in fanciful clothes in *Habiti antichi e moderni di tutto il mondo*.

In the following pages, a Japanese costume book picturing the inhabitants of the world will be analysed. It was printed in two editions: Nishikawa Joken's *Shijuni-koku-jinbutsu zusetsu* (*The People of a Myriad Countries*) (1720) and a revised edition by Yamamura Saisuke, *Teisei shijunikoku jinbutsuzusetsu* (*The People of the Forty-Two Countries*) (1801). These books display ninety-five images of men and women from Asia and Europe, dressed in different fashions, from Africa, and from North and South America, sparsely covered with loincloths and feathers. Common features of the European and Japanese costume books are a combination of images and text as well as changes in the iconography and narrative over time. The section addresses the circulation of visual and textual culture between Italy, mainly Venice, and East Asia and questions the parallel developments of a genre shaped by far-reaching networks of communication and exchange.

Cross-Cultural Exchanges: Embassies and Books

Lorenzo Priuli, the Venetian ambassador in Rome, described the hybrid style of the young Japanese in a letter to the Venetian Senate: 'Their dress looks like a sailor's outfit, with large trousers down to the feet, with no turban or long robe over them. They carry a scimitar around the waist and on the right shoulder a cloak with an iron point. They wear a Spanish styled hat with feathers and ruffles. Their complexion and skin colour are ugly' (Berchet, 1877: 21).

An anonymous *Relazione* printed in Bologna in 1585 describes the solemn entrance of the ambassadors in Rome. The Japanese rode on horseback among high-ranking clergy, Swiss guards, and Roman nobles wearing their ceremonial dress:

> White tunics embroidered with foliage and birds in gold and very vivid colours, cut open on the chest and with large sleeves; over this they wore a sort of wide-bottomed jacket of the same fabric, but more exquisite pattern. The dress would have had a long train, had they not lifted it with a rich scarf which hung graciously from their hips, in the shape of a rose. They wore large and short silk trousers, very fine white socks and leather soles tied to their feet with leather straps passing between the big toe and the other toes. They wore no hat, and their very black hair was tied in a ponytail folded back over their shaven foreheads. This extraordinary hairstyle is a unique feature of these people. Around the waist they carried a magnificent sword and a very fine dagger, with a golden handle encrusted with precious stones. (Berchet, 1877: 22)

The pope gave them three thousand scudi for their personal expenses and 'three sorts of very distinguished Italian dresses: a short one and two long ones, in black velvet embroidered with gold and in golden damask with golden lace. He also gave them a long simar to be worn at home, of the same damask' (Guarnieri, 1586: 49). To all four, the pope also gave a golden chain with a medal. The four young lords (*daimyos*) were endowed with the status of citizens and patricians and dressed in Roman clothes, presumably those Gregorio XIII had offered. The Venetian ambassador Priuli wittily observed: 'They are now wearing long Roman clothes lined with gold and look like doctors from Bologna' (Berchet, 1877: 25). Later, the *daimyos* continued on to Venice, where they were received in their Japanese costume by the ninety-five-year-old Doge Niccolò da Ponte.

Alessandro Valignano, father general of the Jesuits in Japan, had planned and organized the mission with two main purposes: to make Japan better known in Europe and thus gain more financial support for the Jesuits in the Far East, and to make Europe, its religion, and its culture better known and appreciated in Japan. There can be little doubt that the envoys put Japan on the map for most Europeans – the oldest map of Japan dating from the 1585 mission is today in the Florence state archive. The samurai brought with them some gifts, among which was the most precious for the pontiff: a pair of screens, or *byobu* (hence the Portuguese or Spanish *biombo*), picturing Azuchi castle and city incorporating features of European architecture, and a preciously ornate kimono and swords offered to the doge in Venice (the Senate ordered that the gifts be stored in the armory – *sala delle armi* – of the Council of Ten, where they were kept until 1773) (Frago Garcia, 1997).

In exchange, the most significant gifts the legates brought back were illustrated books, which were to exert a considerable influence in Japan: Abraham Ortelius' *World Atlas* p – *Theatrum Orbis Terrarum* – and the first three volumes of Braun and Hogenberg's *Civitates Orbis Terrarum*, given to them by the German botanist Melchior Guilandinus, director of the Botanical Garden in Padua. Both works contained the images of cities and peoples around the world (Sullivan, 1989; Mendes Pinto, 1993; Loh, 2013).

After eight years of travel, in March 1591, Valignano led the recently returned envoys back in a lavish procession through the streets of Kyoto to the court of Hideyoshi, the de facto ruler of Japan. In Italy and Europe, the mission of the four Christianized samurai aroused such public interest that already by 1586 some forty-five accounts had been published, mainly in Italy and Spain, but also in France, Germany, and Prague, together with a handful of prints. Before the end of the century, more than seventy publications appeared in various European languages (Boscaro, 1973).

The Young Japanese

Addressing his readers in 1590, Cesare Vecellio expounds on the difficulties he had encountered in obtaining information on the clothing of Asia:

> It was easier for me to discuss the styles of dress of Europe, mostly because I had seen them myself, and, if not, people I could trust had told me about them and recounted what they had seen themselves. Accounts of Asia, in contrast are so uncertain that it is often necessary, because of geographical distance, to listen to people who speak of things they have not seen themselves but have only heard second hand . . . Asia extends to the East Indian Sea and reaches the Indian Ocean, including Japan and the infinite number of islands surrounding it. Now, I have received accurate information about this third part of

> the world from many people who have been there and from people who live in its countries, having carried out careful research myself. So, I will speak of these styles of dress. But I ask that the reader pardon me if I do not describe them fully, as I did the earlier ones.
>
> (Vecellio, 1590: 432 v–433 r; Rosenthal and Jones, 2008: 433)

The image of the young Japanese indeed appeared eight years later in the second edition of the *Habiti*, together with twenty new prints picturing the peoples of America, and, as Section 1 shows, the inhabitants of Scandinavia.

Before the highly popular 1585 visit, few images of the Japanese had circulated in Italy. The literate public had vague notions about Japan, often still based on Marco Polo's descriptions, that were still reported in Benedetto Bordone's lavishly illustrated *Isolario* (Venice, 1534) and Giuseppe Rosaccio's world history *Il Mondo e le sue parti, cioè Asia, Africa, America* (Florence, 1595) (Reichert, 1993; Proust, 1997; De Castro, 2013: 39–93). The earliest reports printed in Italy with descriptions of the Japanese diplomatic delegation do not provide cogent accounts. The Venetian ambassador Priuli pictured the daimyos wearing clothes 'alla marinaresca', with Spanish-style feathered hats, large and long trousers, scimitar, and a cloak with an iron point, or 'alla romana' with long gowns and golden decorations. The contemporary chronicle from Bologna offers some details of a ceremonial dress embroidered with foliage and birds that Vecellio mentioned in his text describing the young daimyo. In the print, the young man holds the train of his dress with one hand, as the Bolognese chronicler observed. However, Vecellio's image of the *giovane giapponese* is puzzling, as it leaves out most of the features described in the short text and adds to the discrepancy between narrative and image (Wilson, 2005: 217–21; Kato, 2007: 227–53). It suggests that Vecellio did not see the Japanese noblemen of the Jesuit delegation. He depicts his young Japanese Christian, probably mixing a variety of written accounts of the visitors' dress (Figure 50). He also says that such men tie on scimitars and daggers, but he gives his figure a slim staff instead. Some of these details may describe the gown and weapons that made their way to the armory in the hall of the Consiglio de' Dieci, but they do not appear in his print. An acute witness of the contemporary chronicle of the city, the artist could not ignore the event especially since – as he writes in the text accompanying the print – the decorated kimono, sword, and dagger that the Japanese had offered the doge were displayed in the *sala* of the Council of Ten for all Venetians to admire and remember.

In addition to the Japanese youth, the 1598 *Habiti* includes another new East Asian plate: the woman from the Molucca islands. With these two new images, Vecellio changed the visual sequence of Asia, which, in the 1590 *Habiti*, displayed costumes of Ethiopians in the court of the great Prester John, the

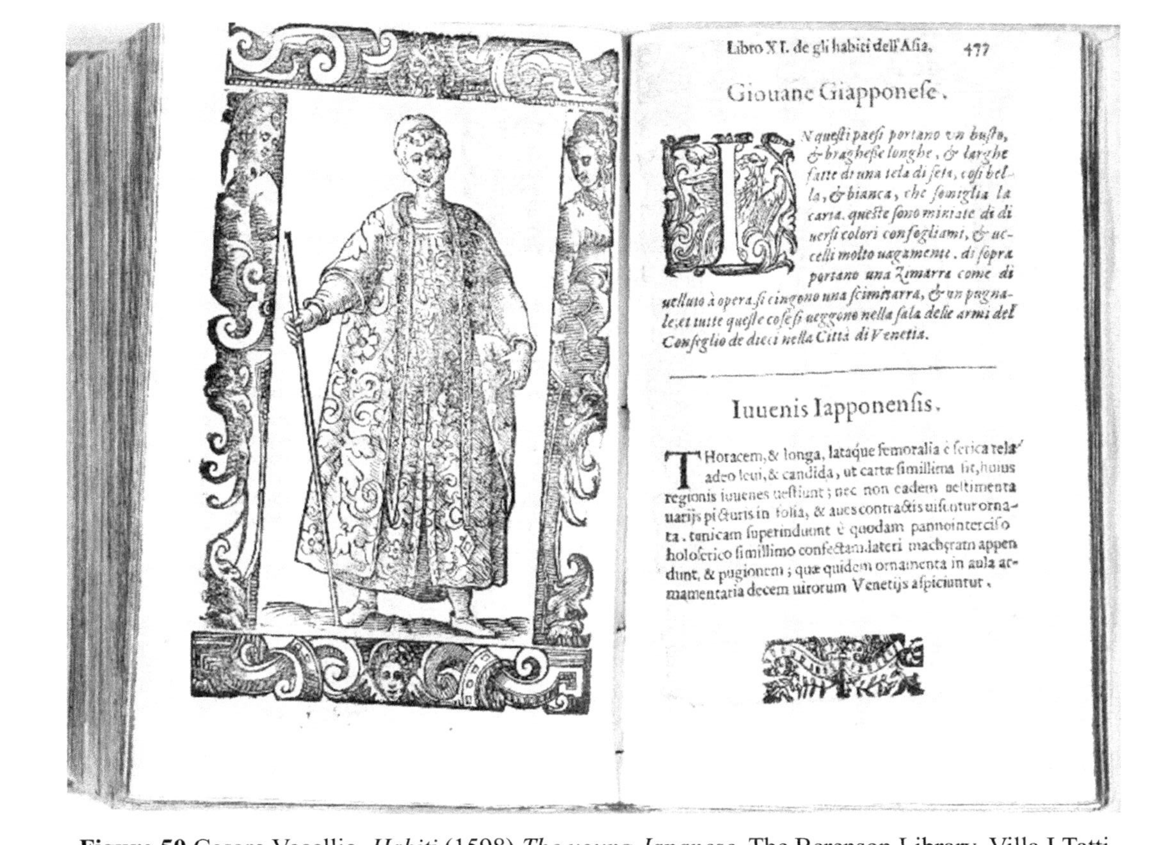

Libro XI. de gli habiti dell'Asia. 477

Giouane Giapponese.

IN questi paesi portano vn busto, & braghesse longhe, & larghe fatte di una tela di seta, cosi bella, & bianca, che somiglia la carta. queste sono miniate di diuersi colori con fogliami, & uccelli molto uagamente. di sopra portano una Zimarra come di uelluto à opera, si cingono una scimitarra, & un pugnale, et tutte queste cose si ueggono nella sala delle armi del Conseglio de dieci nella Città di Venetia.

Iuuenis Iapponensis.

THoracem, & longa, lataque femoralia è serica tela adeo leui, & candida, ut cartæ simillima sit, huius regionis iuuenes uestiunt; nec non eadem uestimenta uarijs picturis in folia, & aues contractis uisuntur ornata. tunicam superinduunt è quodam panno interciso holoserico simillimo confectam. lateri machæram appendunt, & pugionem; quæ quidem ornamenta in aula armamentaria decem uirorum Venetijs aspiciuntur.

Figure 50 Cesare Vecellio, *Habiti* (1598) *The young Japanese*. The Berenson Library, Villa I Tatti

legendary Christian king whose domain was imagined in innumerable lay and religious chronicles to be somewhere between Africa and Asia. From one edition to the next, the Venetian artist replaced these legendary references with updated information about the recently conquered and partly Christianized Pacific islands. The woman from the Moluccas and the Japanese youth embody the space of the Pacific Ocean and are the key to the global dimension of the *Habiti* in Vecellio's panoptic view of the clothed bodies of the people of the world, beginning with ancient Rome, progressing through Christianity and modernity (which peaks in Venice), and culminating, as it were, with twenty illustrations of men and women from the New World.

Though the first edition included four illustrations of men and women from China directly after India Orientale, the revised 1598 edition has them following the two new figures from the Moluccas and Japan. By this careful placement within his own visual itinerary, Vecellio moved to the Far East from the Pacific, reaching Japan first and then moving towards the Chinese mainland. This was the Franciscan and Augustinian missionary route from the New World to Asia across the Pacific, where Japan was the northern point of arrival after the so-called Islands of India – that is, Moluccas, Philippines, and Sunda. Only in Vecellio's second edition does the new Hispanic route to the Far East become visible, in both text and image, and thus the Pacific Ocean becomes a space in and of itself.

Information about these newly discovered islands was circulating in Venice. In 1554, Ramusio had published the first volume of his *Navigazioni e viaggi*, printing Ludovico di Varthema's travelogue to the spice islands in the Pacific, which included the first published description of the isles of Maluch (Ramusio, 1978: 863–5). New knowledge about China was also circulating in Venice, where Juan Gonzales de Mendoza's *Historia della China* was printed in 1586, and in Rome, just as the Japanese mission was arriving in Italy, introducing the young daimyos to those cities (Gonzales de Mendoza, 1586). The *Historia della China* enjoyed such success on the book market that it warranted the publication of two later Venetian editions in 1588 and 1590.

Gonzales de Mendoza was an Augustinian friar from Mexico who wrote using missionary sources that describe Augustinian and Franciscan missionaries crossing the Pacific Ocean from Mexico, landing in the Philippines, and from there travelling to Japan. He also used a wealth of original Chinese sources translated into Spanish by Christianized Chinese in the Philippines. His bestselling history of China is Vecellio's main source on China in the first (1590) *Habiti*, and on China and Japan in the second (1598). Warning his readers that contemporary notions of the Far East were hazy, the artist drew four Chinese costumes that appear in both editions of his work: two for women (a noble matron and a noble woman) and two for men (a noble man and a man of middle standing). Though it is difficult to trace visual models for these images, the 1590 text repeats word for word several quotes from Mendoza's *Historia*. Vecellio transcribed extended passages that detail marriage and sexual customs, food, clothing, bodily manipulations – the binding of women's feet – political practices, religious beliefs, and the wealth of decorations (paintings, sculptures, carvings) on Chinese furniture and bedsteads. Mendoza's *Historia* was new on the market and suggested ways of conceptualizing and constructing geographical space through European expansion, trade, and evangelization on a global scale. Vecellio's staging of the costumes of the non-Western world acknowledged this global circulation of texts across transcontinental diplomatic and missionary connections. These passed through Italy, especially Venice, which, as a centre of production and trade as well as an editorial market, retained crucial interests in the Ottoman Empire and the Far East. Books, maps, and clothing not only migrated towards Europe, but, as we shall see in the following pages, moved east as well when the encounter and violent rejection of Catholic European countries marked the so- called Christian century (1540–1640) in Japan.

Nanban World Maps

Art historians have discussed the cross-cultural exchanges that influenced the production of 'Nanban' art in Japan between the sixteenth and seventeenth centuries. The expression refers to a variety of artistic productions that arose from the interactions between Japan and the Iberian world during the 'Christian century'. In Japanese, the word Nanban – 'Southern Barbarians' – included Portuguese merchants and missionaries arriving in Nagasaki in the 1540s as well as Spaniards who came from the Philippines and Italian Jesuits from Europe. Nanban art comprises three broad categories (Loh, 2013). The first groups Christian works produced by Japanese artists under the supervision of Jesuit missionaries. The second includes large folding screens depicting the *Arrival of the Southern Barbarians* (Figure 51). The ninety-three known screens include a large Portuguese trading ship downloading exotic merchandise in a Japanese port town. European traders and mariners are depicted with large noses and wearing colourful trousers in the middle of a bustling crowd of black slaves, missionaries, and exotic animals under the eyes of Japanese onlookers.

The third category comprises folding screens with painted European world maps (Figure 52). The twenty-two known examples are painted in ink, colour,

Figure 51 Lisbon, Museu Nacional de Arte Antiga, *Japanese Screen picturing the arrival of the Southern Barbarians.*

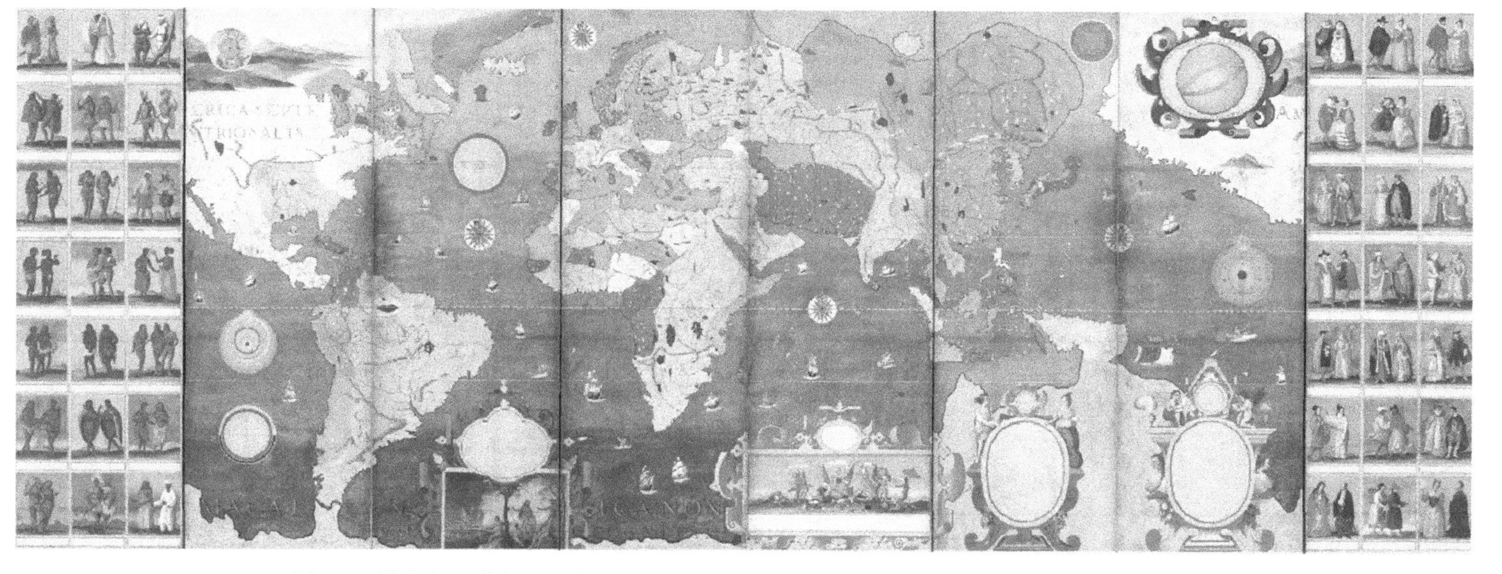

Figure 52 *Map of the World*. Japan, seventeenth century (Imperial Household Agency)

and gold leaf on paper and were created in pairs with six to eight parts that range from 68 to 204 centimeters in height and from 226.5 to 447 centimeters in width. These Nanban world map screens constitute the most nuanced and complex of all objects epitomizing the initial encounter between Japan and Europe during the 1540s through to 1640s (Loh, 2013: 243). They became fashionable in Japan among wealthy merchants involved in maritime trade in coastal port towns and in growing urban centres such as Osaka and Edo. This emerging class commissioned the Nanban world maps for display in their opulent households, as well as for gifts. The fashion was so widespread that Francesco Neretti, a Tuscan merchant who had lived for thirty-eight years in China and Japan, offered Grand Duke Cosimo III de' Medici two painted bamboo screens from Macao, now lost or untraced, picturing the cities of Beijing and Canton (ASF, *Mediceo del Principato* 5080, *c.*464, 8 January 1617).

In Japan, the Portuguese and Italian Jesuits began to encourage a local artistic production aimed at proselytizing, teaching, and spreading European knowledge. Among the many hybrid religious and secular artifacts produced by Jesuit and Japanese artists (the Niccolò and Kano schools), world maps framed with the representation of world people have attracted scholarly attention (Toby, 1998, 2001b). Most surprisingly, however, the representations of peoples from around the world have not been the subject of an extended analysis, whereas the spatial setting on these maps has been mainly analysed in reference to European cartography (Unno, 1994). I focus on these figures, drawing connections with the production of world maps and books of costumes printed in Europe and Japan.

Studies have shown that a limited number of European prints influenced the images on the Japanese world map screens. Some illustrated books imported from Europe as diplomatic gifts including Ortelius' *Theatrum Orbis Terrarum*, the first three volumes of Braun and Hogenberg's *Civitates Orbis Terrarum*, and Dutch maps decorated with frames representing world peoples in couples. The Dutch cartographer Jodocus Hondius (1563–1611) seems to have been the first map-maker to include a frame featuring the people of the world around a map (Sullivan, 1989; Mendes Pinto, 1993; Loh 2013: 37). All Western maps, whether of Jesuit or Dutch origin, presented a striking contrast to contemporary Japanese beliefs that the earth consisted of only three great land masses: India, China, and Japan. This reflects the framework of a Buddhist spiritual topography that inspired the production of the Gyoki-zu maps in which Japan is rendered through a series of rounded forms with indistinct coastlines. Maps combining the traditional rounded land masses framed by images of world peoples provide an interesting example of the hybridization processes taking place.

In 1639, approximately fifty years following the return of the Japanese delegation, the Jesuits and all missionary orders were expelled from Japan. Christianity was banned and persecuted, and only the Dutch, in the enclosed merchant community of Deshima in Nagasaki, were allowed to trade with the shogunate. As recent research has confirmed, notwithstanding the official isolationist policy and the formal ban on the import of foreign books, a clandestine manuscript and book circulation continued from China into Japan. In the Far East, the representation of the peoples of the world as largely monstrous and imaginary had a long-standing tradition and derived from Chinese images, known as *Shan-hai ching*, that first described the varieties of peoples inhabiting the world. The illustrations included deformed animals, birds, fish, and human beings. These were partly absorbed into the Pacific-centred map of the world drawn by the Jesuit Matteo Ricci and exported to Japan, where it was printed in Nagasaki in 1645 (Sato, 1996: 44–63). Commonly known as the *Bankoku jinbutzu zu* (Pictures of the Peoples of a Myriad Countries), it is the first European-derived map published in Japan (Figure 53). Significantly, it represents how quickly Japanese artists had adapted European map imagery for popular audiences by the middle of the seventeenth century. The *Bankoku* bears a legend at the top, which reads as follows:

> The world is broad; the variety of its peoples is without end. Just as its countries differ, the peoples are likewise different in appearance: some are tall, some are short; they appear in paired opposites: black and white; male and female. If we represent their body types as specimens, this is what they are generally like. One can distinguish at a glance their systems of clothing and headgear, the manufacture of their bows, swords, and weapons. One can instantly distinguish the quality of each people in the regions of the world. We have prepared this chart solely that it may serve as an aid to the investigation of things and accomplishment of knowledge.

In a simple yet effective language, this legend provides us with the paradigm that will shape all representations of the forty-two peoples of the world (Toby, 1998:19–44). The variety of the world is spelled out through the description of body types based on height, colour, and gender as well as each people's material culture: clothing, headgear, and the manufacture of weapons. In the framework of a civilizing discourse, the figures are arranged in couples according to the hierarchy of values of a sixteenth-century European and to the amount and style of clothes worn, skin colour, tattoos, animal products, and feathers. The Japanese couple is situated in a dominant position on the top right-hand side of the chart, and at its antipodal point, on the bottom right-hand side of the grid, a roughly outlined Brazilian couple stands beside an open grated fire where

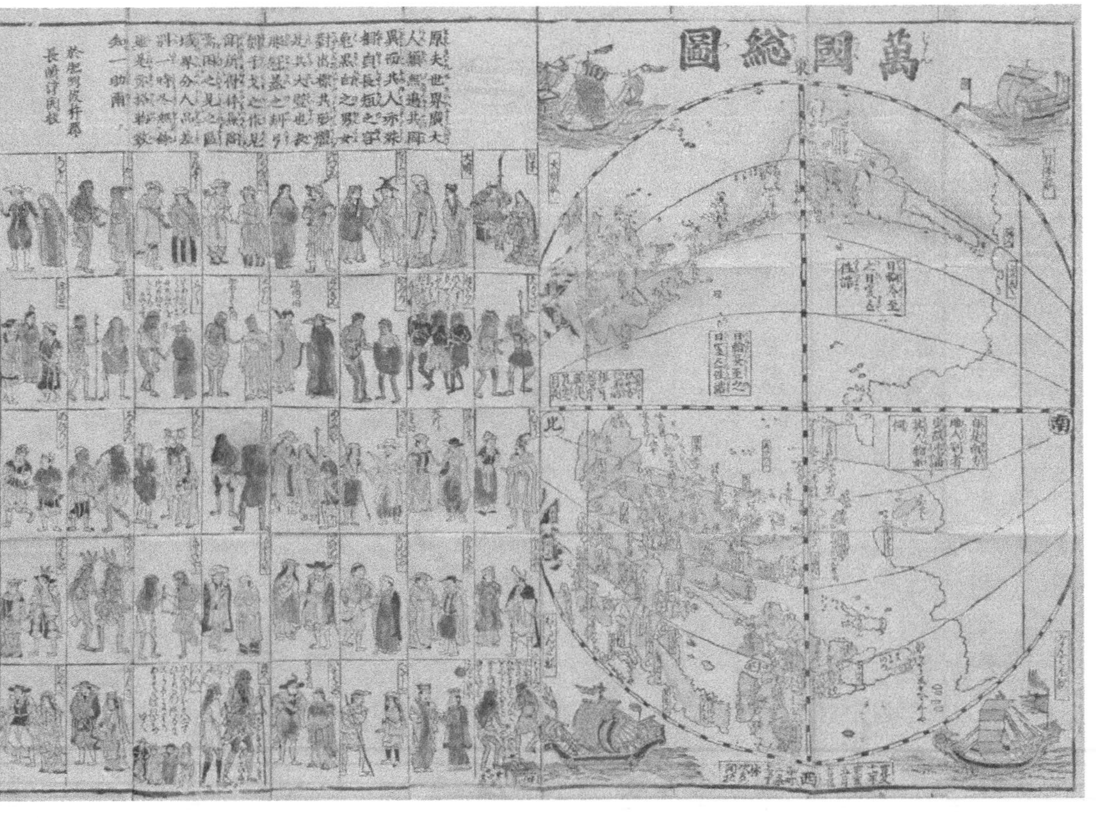

Figure 53 *Bankoku Sozu* 1671. Courtesy of the Bayerische Staatsbibliothek, Munich

human limbs are roasting, epitomizing the opposite poles of civility and barbarism.

The 1645 *Bankoku* offered on the small and handy format of a single sheet the same Westernized representation of the world and its inhabitants pictured on the large folding screens. It gained immediate popular success and circulated among the urban reading public who had no access to the lavishly ornate folding screens but shared the emergence of a new geographical consciousness in Tokugawa Japan. The *Bankoku* was incessantly republished: five new editions appeared between 1645 and 1652, smaller versions with illustrations of world people were printed in encyclopedias and eight versions of the map appeared between 1693 and 1713. It was intended as a work of entertainment and decoration, not as a source for reliable cartographic information. Its reception among a broad reading audience influenced changes in format, place names, and colour. A conflation of European, Chinese, and Japanese sources contributed to the making of the 1645 *Bankoku* and to its lasting success in the editorial market (Shintaro Ayusawa, 1964: 275–94; Hung-kay-Luk, 1977: 58–84). Focussing our attention on its display of world peoples, we have to keep in mind that these replicated in a more rudimentary style the icons decorating the large Momoyama (1573–1615) and Edo (1615–1868) folding screens that are today in the Nanban Bunka-kan museum in Osaka, the Idemitsu Museum of Arts, and the Imperial Household Agency in Tokyo. This migration of images from the screens to the 1645 *Bankoku* sheds light on the already mentioned transfer into a cheaper and popular format of images, which originated in and were accessible to the milieu of the social and political élites. It also confirms the connection between the representation of bodies and geographical knowledge within a circulation and transfer of books and maps from Europe to Japan. The *Bankoku* translated visually a new emerging consciousness of the global dimension of the world as a consequence of the arrival of Europeans in Japan and suggests 'an anthropology of alterities evocative of the panoptic posture' which resonates with the display of identities on the theater of the modern world in European costume books (Toby, 1998: 21). Scholarship unanimously points to the impact of the *Nanban* world view as a turning point in the construction of geographical space (Toby, 1998, 2001: 17; Nenzi, 2008).

Japanese Costume Books: Nishikawa Joken, *The People of the Forty-Two Countries*

The following paragraphs will turn to a new text from a later period: *The People of the Forty-Two Countries*, a Japanese costume book printed in 1720 and revised in 1801, and to its two authors, Nishikawa Joken and Yamamura

Saisuke. The main source for the images is the 1645 *Bankoku*. Comparing the prints of the two editions of the Japanese costume book will shed light on visual and textual continuities and changes, as well as on the adoption and local readaptation of European cultural traditions.

While large-scale maps were reproduced on hanging scrolls and tatami floors and could be unrolled and spread out, images of world people also suggested a more personal intimate enjoyment, and they were displayed in book form or on a hand scroll. These two formats encouraged a different aesthetic and narrative appreciation of the pictorial sequence, as the hand scroll revealed images slowly, unrolling in gradual progression with images flowing into one another (Unno, 1994: 346–477). The book format framed images in a rigid visual order, separating one sheet from the next and clearly distinguishing each image from the next one. When hand scrolls were turned into printed books, the flowing representation of the hand scroll did not always fit the page format.

Nishikawa Joken, a merchant and astronomer from Nagasaki, was an eighteenth-century encyclopedist and one of the most renowned Japanese geographers of his time. He was also one of the most widely read and published popular writers on morals among merchants in the Tokugawa era, drawing from Neo-Confucianism the idea of a natural universal reason that gave all human beings a common identity in humankind. Joken prompted values empowering human activity in ordinary life and viewed merchants as those who could enhance the nation's well-being through the circulation of social wealth, which legitimized a just profit (Tetsuo Najita, 1987: 25). In 1714, he wrote the *People of the Forty-Two Countries* (Figures 54 and 55). Without quoting his sources because of the prohibition of importing foreign books into Japan, he borrowed extensively from the Italian Jesuit tradition rooted in Ricci's writings, using and paraphrasing Giulio Aleni's world geography and testifying to the crucial importance of the clandestine circulation of international scientific literature among the intellectuals of the Edo period. He inaugurated the new book format, where a brief text commented the images of the forty-two peoples of the world. Addressing his readers, he anticipates what his book offers: pictures, information about world peoples, and illustrations representing them. It offers useful knowledge to those interested in trade, fashion, and learning. 'The images you will see in this book introduce the redhead barbarians (the Dutch). These illustrations may serve commercial gains, fashion, or a serious desire for knowledge.'

Reflecting on these foreign customs will allow readers to distinguish between good and evil, justice and injustice, in each of the forty-two countries. Joken clearly distinguishes between 'Qing' and 'Ming' – that is, between Chinese who had or had not adopted Manchu customs. He introduces this distinction, dating it back to the dramatic revolution of 1644 in China when the Manchus prevailed

Figure 54 Nishikawa Joken, *People of the Forty-Two Countries* (1720) *Man and Woman from Italy*. Courtesy of the C. V. Starr East Asian Library, University of California at Berkeley

Figure 55 Nishikawa Joken, *People of the Forty-Two Countries* (1720) *A Dutch Family*. Courtesy of the C. V. Starr East Asian Library, University of California at Berkeley

over the ancient Ming dynasty. Breaking away from the 1645 *Bankoku*, which pictured only the Ming, Joken's text and images offer an original contribution, highlighting dynastic change and connecting it to a landmark historical event. Insisting on China's new dynasty and Manchu conquest underlined Japan's interest in acquiring a new centrality in East Asia after the Mongol dynasty conquered the Chinese, who had therefore lost their leading position.

Other new elements in Joken's volume are the inclusion of the people from Ryukyu, distinct from Chinese and Japanese, the exclusion of Ezo (nowadays Hokkaido), and the division of the world into five continents. Magellanica, the fifth continent, is at times identified with the land of the giants, as in the *Bankoku*, or with the Patagon, a tribe in the extreme southern region of the American continent (Toby, 2001: 31). No image of Japanese people or of Japanese clothing appears in this book, which only pictures others from near and far away. The table of contents lists twenty-one countries in Asia, four in Africa, ten in Europe (including Russia and Ukraine), and five in America. Dwarfs from Siberia and giants from Magellanica appear at the end. The first volume on the East acknowledges local costumes and customs as part of a dynastic history with a keen attention to the origin, antiquity, and transformation of place names in Chinese, Japanese, local, and, at times, European languages. The text mentions the Mughal, Chinese, and Persian Empires. Macao, with a man and woman dressed in the Portuguese fashion, concludes the first volume.

Joken's second volume opens with Turkey and proceeds to islands in Indonesia. It then moves to Africa, described as a region inside 'Limia' – probably 'Libya', from classical sources circulating in European cartography and costume books – and Russia, described as a very cold country with an imposing military might. Notions about Western Europe are vague: Denmark is described as bordering the Mediterranean in its southern part, while its northern boundaries touch the North Pole. Next come Hungary, Poland, Italy, Germany, France, the Netherlands, and England.

Comparing these images with those of the 1645 *Bankoku*, both continuities and discontinuities appear. While icons of the ten European couples *in Europe* largely replicate the fancy clothes, headgear, and gestures in the earlier volume, Joken's narrative acknowledges the global presence of Europeans *outside of Europe*. He mentions Dutch traders in Taiwan (originally Takasago), Java, and some Indonesian islands; the Portuguese in India, China, and Brazil; and the Spaniards in the Philippines and Peru. He calls attention to the military strength of Turks and Russians (Jardine and Brotton, 2000: 78; Screech, 2011: 304–9). Joken also points to the global spread of religion – the 'false doctrine' of Catholicism – as a consequence of Spanish and Portuguese expansion in the Far East. The word for 'false doctrine' is *jaho* and it refers to a doctrine or law

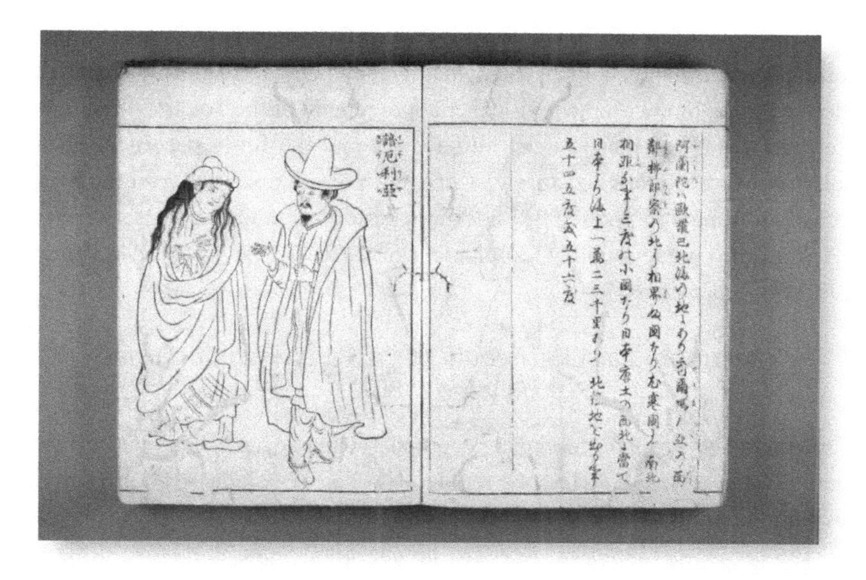

Figure 56 Nishikawa Joken, *People of the Forty-Two Countries* (1720), *Man and Woman from Macao*. Courtesy of the C. V. Starr East Asian Library, University of California at Berkeley

contrary to Buddhist precepts. Joken describes Luzon, the main island of the Philippines, as a place which 'has recently been assimilated to those countries under the influence of the false doctrines and a high number of its dwellers have converted'. In Macao and Goa, they are adopting the same false beliefs 'and even though Macao is in the middle of the seas south of China, Goa in the southern region of India and Portugal is a kingdom in Europe, we can say that their customs and habits are very similar' he concludes. Though Spaniards and Portuguese are mentioned, they are visually excluded, emphasizing a Japanese perspective, which suppresses the presence of Iberians, who were still portrayed in the *Bankoku*. Significantly, Joken portrays a woman and man from Macao wearing Portuguese clothing (Figure 56).

Joken draws a transcontinental Catholic connection between Macao, Goa, and Portugal. Christianity as a globalizing and threatening set of values, beliefs, and practices is a cultural feature that intersects the production of knowledge about the people of the world in the 1720 Japanese text.

A host of anti-Christian writings circulating in Japan from the middle of the seventeenth century until well into the eighteenth provide a meaningful context for the perception of the spreading of Christianity as a preparation for a European invasion. Printed and handwritten, these texts were popular anti-Christian tales and horror stories picturing Christianity as a dangerous foreign religion spread by wicked magicians. They were not aimed at the literate public but, with the political encouragement of the Tokugawa shogunate, this narrative reached deep into society and the furthest corners of the country. More effective than anti-Christian persecution, this literature was effective in shaping popular attitudes in a period when the Japanese were cut off from all contacts with the outside world (Ross, 1994: 110–11; Proust, 1997: 93–5; Elisonas, 2007) .

Yamamura Saisuke, *People of the Forty-Two Countries, Revised* (1801)

Yamamura Saisuke, a professional geographer who had translated into Japanese Dutch works on world geography replicated Joken's book on scroll in 1801. In his revision of Joken's book, entitled *Teisei shijunikoku Jinbutsuzusetsu* (*People of the Forty-Two Countries, Revised*) he consulted some thirty-two different kinds of Western sources, completing the largest and most complete study on world geography to appear during the Edo period (Shintaro Ayusawa, 1964: 282–3). In the introduction, he brings to light the workings of an informal network of friends, reading and circulating scrolls which were carefully studied and discussed in domestic settings. While books were mainly borrowed from libraries and indicate a more formal organization of knowledge, scrolls were hand copied and exchanged among a literate society of readers and local scholars that became acquainted with printed works mainly through borrowing, exchange, and the hand drawing of books into scrolls for their own use. Some of these scrolls were passed to publishers who assembled designers, woodcarvers and a printer and produced wood block images for the final prints, in scroll and/ or book format. In this way, official cartography and images of world people gradually filtered through to a broader public (Wigen, 2010: 26).

Saisuke insists on the hybrid nature of his revised edition, influenced by Chinese and Western models. The official interpreter of the Dutch community had written parts of the preface, which the Chinese interpreter then translated into Chinese. The best linguistic skills were indeed found among the five families of hereditary translators retained in Nagasaki by the East India Dutch Company (VOC), and a similar number were employed to negotiate with the Chinese community (Screech, 2002: 15). The *Teisei* is thus situated within the merchant international community of Nagasaki and is a text of commercial geography. It includes the same woodblock prints as the previous seventeenth-century edition, with a revised and enlarged written commentary. In 1801, the ban on the import of foreign books had just been lifted, and that is probably accountable for the richer information circulating in the *Teisei*, compared to the 1720 edition (Wigen, 2010: 89). In the opening paragraphs, Saisuke indeed acknowledges this: 'In the past, as we could not visit all the lands we describe, we have integrated information from western geographies.' The Dutch influenced the illustrations, while the place names come from Ming sources, which include and translate Jesuit knowledge. The text also uses 'current news' and is part of a common trend as 'all countries nowadays certainly have their own works describing foreigners and therefore the one we are now editing is just one of many'.

The scroll opens with three colorful images: two Japanese functionaries, dressed in a black and a blue kimono and a woman wearing the twelve-layered Heian court costume. They reproduce the portraits from *Thirty-Six Poetic Immortals*, a hanging scroll from the mid-thirteenth century picturing Heian court scenes from the Kamakura period (1185–1333) (Liddell, 1989). A unique feature of the *Teisei* is the visual inclusion of the Japanese among the peoples of the world, stressing the centrality of Japan, which opens the visual display on the scroll. The three figures trace images from a 600-year-old source and artistic tradition, in order to legitimize the centrality of Japan in East Asia based on its ancient dynastic culture. The precious textiles, headgear, and multilayered court dress of the woman set them apart from contemporary attire and the dangers of ethnic, religious, and aesthetic contamination. The image constructs the Japanese as structurally linked to their past in splendid isolation and dynastic superiority. This ahistorical condition places them outside of contemporary history – that is, the encounter with Western colonizers – that threatens their very survival, as the text underlines.

The *Tesei* introduces the reader to an overwhelmingly peaceful landscape that depicts the uniqueness of Japan: 'Our country, Japan, is situated in the remote Eastern regions of the globe but has a pleasant climate and a fertile soil. Our clothing, literature and artistic styles are unique and extraordinary. Our generation lives happily and peacefully' (Saisuke, 1802: par. 2).

Reminiscences of the 1645 *Bankoku* resonate in the narrative describing world people as body types, customs, and clothing:

> The continents differ from one another. There are people with black skin, others with curly hair, people who eat men and brand their bodies with fire, other who go about naked because of the heat and drink a lot. Some during the winter produce no cereals and eat the flesh of fish and birds. On the contrary there are those who have all grains and fruits, prepare sake, dress with clothing made with birds' plumage, and protect the skin of their faces. They are bandy legged and do not use bows and arrows.

Moving westwards, the text lists, describes, and illustrates continents, countries, and islands with the clothed and naked bodies of men, women, and children, repeating the pattern found in Joken's 1720 text. Asia is the most highly represented with twenty-two regions, mostly corresponding to the different stages of the expansion of the Chinese Empire; Europe has ten woodcuts, Africa and South America – including Patagonia – four each and North America (i.e., Canada) just one. Continents, regions, and lands appear as parts of past or existing empires (Tracy, 1990; Adshead, 1993; Ropp, 2010). Gone are all references to Christianity and Catholicism, and no image of the Portuguese and Spaniards is included in the section on Europe. The narrative insists on European trade and military expansion from the sixteenth century onwards. Repeating the 1720 text, Spaniards and Portuguese are extensively quoted for their territorial conquests in the Pacific, South America, and Southeast Asia, where Japanese commercial interests and exchanges had been a long-standing tradition since the sixteenth century. The Danes and especially the Dutch are mentioned, with emphasis on their military and commercial bases in South Africa and Southeast Asia. A notion of civilization is introduced in connection with European influence over non-Asian people: Africans and Brazilians are described as having become more civilized in contact with Europeans and the images picture fair-skinned couples or nuclear families instead of cannibals (as Brazilians in the 1645 *Bankoku*). Jesuit sources are explicitly quoted in the text, using Chinese names. Ricci and Aleni are respectively Li and Gai, and their work helps the author to situate and identify Canada, correcting the wrong place name used in the 1720 edition: 'I have read carefully the works of Li and Gai from the Ming period and the term Kanarin does not appear. Kanaada is the word, and it is a large country in the Eastern part of North America, also known as New France.' Ferdinand Verbiest, a Belgian Jesuit writing in Chinese, is also quoted for the description of the Terra Magellanica and its giants. Owing to the lifting of the ban on foreign books, the 1801 edition fully acknowledges Western Jesuit sources, and quotations from Jesuit texts increased and became explicit (Verbiest was not mentioned in 1720).

Repeating the 1720 edition in book format, the 1801 scroll records in detail bodily images of men, women, children, and old people often in couples, but at times in groups of three or more. Their dress is more detailed in the sections on Asia, where material culture provides a livelier setting to the icons. Bizarre clothes, plumes, animal skins characterize non-Asian people pictured mainly as heterosexual couples, as in the long-standing North European tradition that influenced Japanese world maps on folding screens and the *bankoku*. The woodcuts illustrate everyday practices and gestures, and include a variety of objects: baskets, boxes, vases, hats, handkerchiefs, gloves, fans, parasols, jewels, bottles, cups, and weapons (mostly shields and arrows but no firearms) (Schmidt, 2011: 31–57). Clothed and semi naked bodies, objects, and gestures function as metonyms for place, embodying the often ill-defined and highly imaginative geographical space described in the texts. Format constructs sequences: the rigid structure of the page confines bodies in a narrow, separated space, while the scroll opens a larger iconic flexibility and gestures are not cut off by the borders of the book.

A complex, dense, and fascinating intertextuality connects the two Japanese editions (Brosius and Wenzlhuemer, 2011: 3–24). These works from the Edo period have to be situated in an expanding editorial market addressing a wide literate readership. The images of world people also appeared in illustrated encyclopedias and popular handbooks of civilized knowledge, which, amidst a wealth of historical and geographical data, often included a rudimentary world map with illustrations of various actual and imagined peoples. This suggests a high level of literacy, and, as of the middle of the seventeenth century, a lively printing industry as well as a 'transformation in spatial consciousness' (Yonemoto, 2003: 648) that sets the stage for a reflection on parallel developments in European societies (Ikegami, 2005; Berry, 2006).

The Threats of Early Globalization

Analysing Vecellio' s image of a young Japanese man in his 1598 *Habiti* brought to light the far-reaching connections between costume books and albums as a genre stretching beyond Europe and the West. Within this framework, a transcontinental circulation of visual and textual knowledge between Europe and Edo Japan mediated by missionaries, diplomats, scientists, and scholars was revealed. The Pacific Ocean is one of the focal points of these interconnections.

A global transmission and circulation of knowledge is visible in both the Italian and the Japanese books where cartography, ethnography, history, trade, and art converge. A growing consciousness of the world's connectivity is perceivable in all three authors: their texts and images express curiosity, self-awareness, fear, nostalgia, superiority, and what Roger Chartier defined as 'métissages des imaginaires' (Chartier, 2001).

Inacio Moreira, a Portuguese cartographer in the retinue of the Jesuit Valignano visiting the emperor of Japan in 1585, produced a map of the world in 1590 that represented Christian kingdoms coloured in gold and Christian peoples in pagan kingdoms (Headley, 2000: 1149–50). Churches and crosses chart the progression of Christianity worldwide. Intended to accelerate the conversion of the Japanese, the map portrayed a global vision of contemporary Christianity in the shape of an advancing Empire of the Cross in non-Western territories. It anticipated the fears of a Western invasion of the Far East that

Joken and Yamamura's image of the Portuguese couple in Canton epitomized in their costume books.

Concluding Remarks

Sidestepping a history of fashion, this book analyses the rich source material that costume books and albums provide from the standpoint of the global circulation and transfer of textual and visual knowledge. In so doing, the mobility of people and things – travel, migration, commerce, colonization, Christianization – takes centre stage. All three sections shed light on the contacts, exchanges, and cultural translations that hybridize the Renaissance genre of costume books with local visual traditions in multiethnic and multi-religious contexts. This introduces a new perspective that decenters the Italian and European Renaissances from unexpected entry points and margins – the island of Chios, Finland, the Balkans, Japan – giving pride of place to the gaze of less-known and extra European authors, geographers, and printers whose work broke the monopoly of the Western discourse. I argue that these sources question change, transformation, and hybridity. Costume books and albums are not a static medium: they are shaped by processes of accumulation, repetition, visual and textual inclusion and exclusion, as well as by the social and cultural practices that define their contexts of production, acquisition, and reception. Many underwent substantial transformations through changing ownership and taste: the multiple uses and meanings they acquired in the hands of collectors such as Vincenzo Giustiniani, Franz Taeschner, Richard Bull, and Frederick Stibbert are of crucial importance.

Agency and choice shape the narrative of this Element, which focusses on individual profiles across far-reaching contacts: diplomats bringing gifts from Venice to Istanbul and from Japan to Europe, missionaries translating geographical and scientific knowledge, collectors, artists, and travellers negotiating visual and textual traditions across linguistic, religious, political, and ethnic borders. Within these networks, we need to acknowledge relations between artists and patrons. Vecellio gathered his main sources in Count Piloni's library, whose volumes he decorated and perused. The costume album that Pomarancio made for Vincenzo Giustiniani traced widely circulating images, yet resignified them through the subject position and experience of his patron. Albums suited these flexible practices of juxtaposition, which gave a new meaning to stereotypical icons available in printed books.

Cesare Vecellio and the two editions of his *Habiti antichi e moderni* (Venice, 1590 and 1598) are the *fil rouge* of the narrative. The *Habiti* functioned as a 'contact zone' that selectively appropriated and translated, in the tradition of the costume book, several European bestsellers published in late Renaissance Venice. An extraordinary capacity to adapt to the new culture of space circulating in Venice marks the major changes introduced in the second edition that provided links to a transcontinental production of texts and images across the Pacific and into the Far East. These cross-cultural borrowings and visual adaptations from Western sources – Olaus Magnus, Nicolas de Nicolay – Ottoman costume albums, and Japanese maps, scrolls, and books were not neutral. Dress epitomized the assimilation of native populations, strategies of colonization and resistance, and refusal to convert to Islam or Christianity.

In a wider historiographical framework, costume albums and books are analysed as flexible, movable, and versatile media. Defined by their mutability, they corresponded to a new consciousness of space and spatial relations, shaped by early modern geography, and addressed processes of cultural globalization in geopolitical areas increasingly subject to the pressure of European imperialisms and Roman universalism. They thus appear as both products of global connections and as themselves shaping new consciousness of connections. Staging the clothing of the world revealed the global tensions that shaped the early modern world. Dress was the micro-historical format that embodied them.

Bibliography

Manuscript Sources

Florence, Archivio di Stato. *Mediceo del Principato*, F. 5080.

Florence, Gabinetto dei Disegni e delle Stampe degli Uffizi. Cristofano Roncalli, il Pomarancio, *Disegni di Figura*, dal 2968 al 3062.

Primary Sources

Alt-Stambuler Hof-Und Volksleben. Ein Turkisches Miniaturenalbum Aus Dem 17 Jahrhundert Veroffentlicht von Franz Taeschner. (1925). Hannover: Orient-Buchhandlung Heinz Lafaire.

A Series of Prints and Drawings Serving to Illustrate the Modes and Fashions of Ancient and Modern Dresses in Different Parts of the World. (1792). Newport, Isle of Wight: Albin Press.

Bassano, Luigi. (1545). *I costumi et i modi particolari de la vita de' Turchi*. Rome: G. A. Dossena.

Belon, Pierre. (1587). *Observations de plusieurs singularités & choses mémorables, trouvées en Grèce, Asie, Judée, Egypte, Arabie & autres pays étranges*. Paris: À l'enseigne du Pelican.

Berchet, Guglielmo. (1877). *Le antiche ambasciate giapponesi in Italia*. Venice.

Bertelli, Ferdinando. (1563). *Omnium fere gentium nostrae aetatis habitus, numquam ante hac aediti*. Venice: Ferdinando Bertelli.

Bertelli, Pietro. (1589–96). *Diversarum nationum habitus*. Padua: Pietro Bertelli and Alcia Alciato.

Boissard, Jean Jacques. (1581). *Habitus variarum orbis gentium*. Mechlin.

Bordone, Benedetto. (1534). *Isolario*. Venice.

Botero, Giuseppe. (2015). *Le Relazioni Universali*. Vol. 1. Alice Raviola, ed. Turin: Nino Aragno editore.

Bruyn, Abraham de. (1581). *Omnium pene Europae, Asiae, Aphricae atque Americae gentium habitus*. Antwerp: M. Colyn.

Deserps, Francois. (2001). *A Collection of the Various Styles of Clothing which are presently worn in countries of Europe, Asia, Africa, and the savage islands, all realistically depicted* [1562]. Sarah Shannon, trans. and ed. Minneapolis, MN: James Ford Bell Library.

Ghislain de Busbecq, Ogier. (2010). *Travels into Turkey* [1744]. London: ECCO Eighteenth Century Collections Online Print Editions.

Gois, Damiao da. (1540). *Deploratio Lappianae Gentis*. Lovanii.

Gonzalez de Mendoza, Giovanni. (1586). *Della Historia della China*. Venice: Andrea Muschio.

Grassi, Bartolomeo. (1585). *Dei veri ritratti degl'habiti di tutte le parti del mondo*. Rome: Bartolomeo Grassi.

Kaan Nagata. (1854). *Kaigai jinbutsu shu*. Kaei7.

Magnus, Olaus. (1555). *Historia de Gentibus Septentrionalibus*. Rome: Giovanni Viotti.

Magnus, Olaus. (1565). *Historia delle genti et della natura delle cose settentrionali*. Venice: Giunti.

Menavino, Antonio. (1548). *Trattato de costumi et vita de Turchi*. Florence: Torrentino.

Nicolay, Nicolas de. (1580). *Le navigationi et viaggi, fatti nella Turchia di Nicolo de Nicolai del Delfinato, con diverse singolarità viste & osservate in quelle parti dall'autore. Nuovamente tradotto di francese in italiano da Francesco Flori da Lilla, aritmetico. Con sessantasette figure naturali, si d'huomini come di donne*. Venice: Francesco Ziletti.

Nicolay, Nicolas de. (1989). *Dans l'Empire de Soliman le Magnifique*, eds. Marie-Christine Gomez-Géraud et Stépane Yérasimos. Presses du CNRS: Paris.

Nishikawa Joken. (1720). *Shijuni-koku jinbutsu zusetsu*. Tobukoto: Einbaken Zohan, Kyoho. Archive.wul.waseda.ac.jp/kosho/ni16/ni16_02281

The Pilgrim: The Journeys of Pietro Della Valle. (1989). George Bull, ed. London: Folio Society.

Ramusio, Giovanni Battista. (1978–88). *Navigazioni e Viaggi*. 6 vols. Marica Milanesi, ed. Torino: Einaudi.

Rosaccio, Giuseppe. (1595). *Il Mondo e le sue parti, cioe' Europa, Asia, Africa e America*. Florence: Francesco Tosi.

Storia D'Olao Magno arcivescovo d'Uspali, de' Costumi de' Popoli Settentrionali tradotta per M. Remigio fiorentino. (1551). Venice: Francesco Bindoni.

Ticozzi, Stefano. (1817). *Vite de' pittori Vecelli di Cadore*. Milano: Stella.

Travels in the Levant: The Observations of Pierre Belon of Le Mans on Many Singularities and Memorable Things Found in Greece, Turkey, Judaea, Egypt, Arabia and Other Foreign Countries (1553). Text established and presented by Alexandra Merle. English translation by James Hogarth. Kilkerran, Scotland: Hardinge Simpole, 2012.

The Travels of Peter Mundy in Europe and Asia 1608–1667. Travels in Europe, vol. 1 (1907). Richard Carnac Temple, ed. Cambridge: Hakluyt Society. www.Bibliolife.com/opensource

Vecellio, Cesare. (1590). *De gli habiti antichi, et moderni di diverse parti del mondo libri due, fatti da C.V. e con discorsi da lui dichiarati*. Venice: Damian Zenaro.

Vecellio, Cesare. (1598). *Habiti antichi et moderni di tutto il mondo; di nuovo accresciuti di molte figure*. Venice: Gio. Bernardo Sessa.

Weiditz, Christoph. (1994). *Authentic Everyday Dress of the Renaissance: All 154 Plates from the 'Trachtenbuch'*. Theodor Kampe, ed. Toronto: Dover.

Yamamura Saisuke. (1801). *Teisei shijunikoku Jinbutsuzusetsu*. archive.wul. waseda.ac.jp/kosho/bunko 08/bunko08_a0240

Secondary Sources

Abulafia, David. (2008). *The Discovery of Mankind*. New Haven, CT: Yale University Press.

Ådahl, Karin. (2006). *The Sultan's Procession: The Swedish Embassy to Sultan Mehmed IV in 1657–1658 and the Rålamb Paintings*. Istanbul: Swedish Research Institute in Istanbul.

Adshead, S. A. M. (1993). *Central Asia in World History*. London: Palgrave Macmillan.

Alfonso, Luis U. (2016). 'Patterns of Artistic Hybridization in the Early Protoglobalization Period'. *Journal of World History* 27: 215–53.

Ambrosini, Federica. (1981). '"Descrittioni del mondo" nelle case venete del XVI e XVII secolo'. *Archivio Veneto* 5(11): 67–79.

Ambrosini Massari, Anna Maria. (2017). 'Roncalli, Cristoforo, detto Pomarancio'. In *Dizionario Biografico degli Italiani*. Rome: Ad vocem: 88.

Arbel, Benjamin. (1996). 'Colonie d'Oltremare'. In Alberti Tenenti and Ugo Tucci, eds. *Storia di Venezia dalle origini alla caduta della Serenissima, vol.* V*: Il Rinascimento. Società ed economia*. Rome: Istituto della Enciclopedia Italiana: 947–85.

Arbel, Benjamin. (2013). 'Venice's Maritime Empire in the Early Modern Period'. In Eric R. Dursteler, ed. *A Companion to Venetian History, 1400–1797*. Leiden: Brill: 125–253.

Bentley, Jerry H. (2012). 'Cultural Exchanges in World History'. In Jerry H. Bentley ed., *The Oxford Handbook of World History Online*. London: Oxford University Press: 1–18.. www.oxfordhandbooks.com. https:doi.org/10.1093/oxfordhb/9780199235810.013.0020

Berry, Mary Elisabeth. (2006). *Japan in Print: Information and Nation in the Early Modern Period*. Los Angeles: University of California Press.

Bertelli, Sergio. (2004). *Trittico: Lucca, Ragusa, Boston: Tre città mercantili tra Cinque e Seicento*. Roma: Donzelli.

Bizoni, Bernardo. (1942). *Europa Milleseicentosei*, Anna Banti, ed. Milano-Roma: Rizzoli.

Blanc, Odile (1995). 'Images du monde et portraits d'habits: Les recueils de costumes à la Renaissance'. *Bulletin du bibliophile* 2: 221–61.

Bleichmar, Daniela. (2011). 'Seeing the World in a Room: Looking at Exotica in Early Modern Collections'. In Daniela Bleichmar and Peter C. Mancall, eds. *Collecting across Cultures*. Philadelphia: Pennsylvania University Press: 15–30.

Bleichmar, Daniela, and Mancall, Peter C. (eds.). (2011). *Collecting across Cultures*. Philadelphia: Pennsylvania University Press.

Born, Robert. (2011). Mapping Transylvania As a Multiethnic and Multiconfessional Region in Costume Books (17th–19th Centuries). In Constanta Vintila-Ghitulescu, ed. *From Traditional Attire to Modern Dress*. Newcastle: Cambridge Scholars: 52–82.

Boscaro, Adriana. (1973). *Sixteenth-Century European Printed Works on the First Japanese Mission to Europe: A Descriptive Bibliography*. Leiden: Brill.

Boscaro, Adriana. (2008). *Ventura e sventura dei Gesuiti in Giappone (1549–1639)*. Venice: Libreria Editrice Cafoscarina.

Boxer, Charles S. (1951). *The Christian Century in Japan, 1549–1650*. Berkeley: University of California Press.

Brafman, David. (2009). 'Facing East: The Western View of Islam in Nicolas de Nicolay's "Travels in Turkey"'. *Getty Research Journal* 1:153–60.

Brook, Timothy. (2008). *Vermeer's Hat: The Seventeenth Century and the Dawn of the Global World*. New York: Bloomsbury Press.

Brosius, Christiane, and Wenzlhuemer, Roland (eds.). (2011). *Transcultural Turbulences. Toward a Multi-Sited Reading of Image Flows*, Berlin Heidelberg, 2011: Introduction, 3–24

Brown, Judith. (1994). 'Courtiers and Christians: The First Japanese Emissaries to Europe', *Renaissance Quarterly* 47: 872–906.

Burke, Peter. (2016). *Hybrid Renaissance: Culture, Language, Architecture*. Budapest: Central European University Press.

Burton, Antoinette. (2012). 'The Body in/as World History'. In Douglas Northrop ed., *A Companion to World History*. Oxford: Oxford University Press: 272–84.

Bury, Michael. (2001). *The Print in Italy: 1550–1620*. London: British Museum Press.

Calvi, Giulia. (2011). *Across Three Empires: Balkan Costumes in XVI Century Europe*. In Constanta Vintila-Ghitulescu, ed., *From Traditional Attire to Modern Dress: Modes of Identification, Modes of Recognition in the Balkans (XVIth–XXth Centuries)*. Newcastle: Cambridge Scholars: 29–51.

Calvi, Giulia. (2017). 'Cultures of Space: Costume Books, Maps and Clothing between Europe and Japan (Sixteenth through Nineteenth Centuries)', *I Tatti Studies in the Italian Renaissance* 20, 2: 331–63.

Calvi, Giulia, and Sebastiani, Silvia (eds.). (2013), 'La Querelle des corps. Acceptions et pratiques dans la formation des sociétés européennes', *L'Atelier du Centre de Recherches historiques* 11 'Introduction'. http://acrh.revues.org/5291

Campbell, Caroline, and Chong, Alan. (2005). *Bellini and the East.* London: National Gallery Company.

Cardini, Chiara, ed. (2001). *La porta d'Oriente. Lettere di Pietro della Valle: Istanbul 1614.* Roma: Città Nuova.

Cavalcaselle, Giovanni Battista. (1878). *Tiziano, la sua vita e i suoi tempi.* Firenze: Le Monnier.

Chartier, Roger. (2001). 'La conscience de la globalité (commentaire)'. *Annales: Histoire, Sciences Sociales* 56: 119–23.

Chiappini di Sorio, Ileana. (1983). *Cristoforo Roncalli detto il Pomarancio.* In Pietro Zampetti, ed. *I pittori bergamaschi: dal XIII al XIX secolo, Il Seicento.* Bergamo: Bolis.

Cohn, Bernard S. (1996). *Colonialism and Its Forms of Knowledge: The British in India.* Princeton, NJ: Princeton University Press.

Collaço, Gwendolyn. (2017). 'Dressing a City's Demeanour: Ottoman Costume Albums and the Portrayal of Urban Identity in the Early Seventeenth Century', *Textile History* 48: 248–67.

Collaço, Gwendolyn. (2018). 'Albums of Conspicuous Consumption: A Composite Mirror of an 18th-Century Collector's World', *Journal 18*, 6 *Albums*. www.journal18.org/3089

Conley, Tom. (1987). *Early Modern Literature and Cartography: An Overview*, in David Woodward, ed., *The History of Cartography*, vol. 3, part 1, Cartography in the European Renaissance. Chicago: Chicago University Press: 401, 408–9.

Conte, Tiziana (ed.) (2001). *Cesare Vecellio 1521–1601.* Belluno: Provincia di Belluno.

Cooper, Michael (ed.). (1971). *The Southern Barbarians.* Tokyo: Kodansha International.

Cooper, Michael. (2005). *The Japanese Mission to Europe, 1582–1590: The Journey of the Four Samurai Boys through Portugal, Spain and Italy.* Folkestone: Waterstones.

Cosgrove, Denis. (1992). 'Mapping New Worlds: Culture and Cartography in Sixteenth Century Venice', *Imago Mundi*, 44: 65–89.

Da Costa Kauffman, Thomas. (2004). *Towards a Geography of Art*. Chicago: University of Chicago Press.

De Anna, Luigi. (1988). *Conoscenza e immagine della Finlandia e del Settentrione nella cultura classico/medievale*. Turku: Turun yliopisto.

De Anna, Luigi. (1994). *Il mito del Nord. Tradizioni classiche e medievali*. Napoli: Liguori.

De Castro, Xavier. (2013). 'Les Premières Cartes du Japon', in X. De Castro (ed.), *La Découverte du Japon par les Européens (1543–1551)*. Paris: Chandeigne, 39–93.

Defert, Daniel. (1984). 'Un genre ethnographique profane au XVIe: les livres d'habits (essai d'ethno-iconographie)'. In Britta Rupp-Eisenreich, ed. *Histoires de l'anthropologie (XVIe–XIXe siécles)*. Paris: Klincksieck, 25–41.

Del Puppo, Dario. (2011). 'All the World Is a Book: Italian Renaissance Printing in a Global Perspective'. *Textual Cultures* 6: 1–22.

Dursteler, Eric R. (2012). 'Speaking in Tongues: Language and Communication in the Early modern Mediterranean'. *Past and Present* 217: 47–77.

Elisonas, George E. (2007). 'Journey to the West'. *Japanese Journal of Religious Studies* 34: 27–66.

Feci, Simona, Bortolotti, Luca, Bruni, Franco. (2001). *Giustiniani, Vincenzo: Dizionario Biografico degli Italiani*. Rome, vol.57 ad vocem.

Fetvaci, Emine. (2011). 'Enriched Narratives and Empowered Images in Seventeenth Century Ottoman Manuscripts'. *Ars Orientalis* 40: 243–66.

Fetvaci, Emine. (2019). *The Album of the World Emperor. Cross-Cultural Collecting and the Art of Album-Making in Seventeenth Century Istanbul*. Princeton, NJ: Princeton University Press.

Findlen, Paula. (1994). *Possessing Nature: Museums, Collecting and Scientific Culture in Early Modern Italy*. Berkeley: University of California Press.

Findlen, Paula (ed.). (2013). *Early Modern Things*. London: Routledge.

Fischer, Erik, with Bencard, Ernest J. and Rasmussen Mikael B. (2009). *Melchior Lorck*. 4 vols. Copenhagen: Vandkunsten.

Fortini Brown, Patricia. (2000). 'Behind the Walls: The Material Culture of Venetian Elites'. In John Martin and Dennis Romano, eds. *Venice Reconsidered: The History and Civilization of an Italian City-State 1297–1797*. Baltimore, MD: Johns Hopkins University Press: 295–338.

Frago Gracia, Juan Antonio. (1997). 'Japonesismos entre Acapulco y Sevilla: sobre biombo, catana y maque', *Boletin de Filologia – Universidad de Chile* 26 (1997): 101–18.

Frazer, Elisabeth A. (2018). 'The Color of the Orient: On Ottoman Costume Albums, European Print Culture and Cross-Cultural Exchange'. In Tara Zanardi and Lynda Clich, eds. *Visual Typologies From the Early*

Modern to the Contemporary: Local Practices and Global Contexts. New York: Routledge: 45–59.

Frazer, Elisabeth A. (2020a). *The Ottoman Costume Album As Mobile Object and Agent of Contact*. In Elisabeth A. Frazer, ed., *The Mobility of People and Things in the Early Modern Mediterranean: The Art of Travel*. New York: Routledge: 91–114.

Frazer, Elisabeth A. (2020b). 'Introduction: The Mobility of People and Things in the Early Modern Mediterranean: The Art of Travel'. In Elisabeth A. Frazer ed., *The Mobility of People and Things in the Early Modern Mediterranean: The Art of Travel*. New York: Routledge: 1–9.

Gerritsen, Anne, and Riello, Giorgio (eds.). (2016). *The Global Lives of Things: The Material Culture of Connections in the Early Modern World*. New York: Routledge.

Gil, Juan. (1991). *Hidalgos y Samurais, Hispania y Japon en los Siglos XVI y XVII*. Madrid: Alianza Universidad.

Gillgren, Peter. (1999). 'The Artist Olaus Magnus: Vision and Illustration'. In *I fratelli Giovanni e Olao Magno: opera e cultura fra due mondi*. Atti del Convegno Internazionale Roma-Farfa: Il Calamo: 147–71.

Gluckman, Dale Carolyn, and SadakoTakeda, Sharon (eds.). (1992). *When Art Became Fashion: Kosode in Edo-Period Japan*. Los Angeles: Weatherhill and Los Angeles County Museum of Art.

Grazioli, Giovanni. (1999). 'I libri dipinti della raccolta Piloni'. *Archivio Storico di Belluno, Feltre e Cadore* 70: 213–14.

Greene, Molly. (2000). *A Shared World: Christians and Muslims in the Early Modern Mediterranean*. Princeton, NJ: Princeton University Press.

Grimes, Katharine I. (2002). 'Dressing the World: Costume Books and Ornamental Cartography in the Age of Exploration'. In Elisabeth Rodini and Elissa B. Weaver eds., *A Well Fashioned Image: Clothing and Costume in European Art 1500–1800*. Chicago: Smart Museum of Art and University of Chicago Press.

Guérin Dalle Mese, Jeannine. (1998). *L'occhio di Cesare Vecellio. Abiti e costumi esotici nel '500*. Alessandria: Edizioni dell'Orso.

Guérin Dalle Mese, Jeannine. (ed.). (2002). *Il vestito e la sua immagine*. Atti del Convegno. Belluno.

Gurkan, Emrah S. (2015). 'Mediating Boundaries: Mediterranean Go-Betweens and Cross-confessional Diplomacy in Constantinople, 1500–1600'. *Journal of Early Modern History* 19: 107–28.

Hanley, Susan B. (1991). 'Tokugawa Society: Material Culture, Standard of Living and Lifestyles'. In *The Cambridge History of Japan*, vol. 4. Cambridge: Cambridge University Press: 660–705.

Hanley, Susan B. (1999). *Everyday Things in Premodern Japan: The Hidden Legacy of Material Culture*. Berkeley: University of California Press.

Harley, John B., and Woodward, David (eds.). (1994). *The History of Cartography*, Vol. 2, Book 2 Appendix 11.4 'Classification of the Namban-Style World Maps'. Chicago: Chicago University Press.

Harley, John B. (2001). *The New Nature of Maps: Essays in the History of Cartography*. Baltimore, MD: Johns Hopkins University Press.

Haskell, Francis. (1980). *Patrons and Painters: A Study in the Relations Between Italian Art and Society in the Baroque*. New Haven, CT: Yale University Press.

Headley, John M. (1997). 'The Sixteenth-Century Venetian Celebration of the Earth's Total Habitability: The Issue of the Fully Habitable World for Renaissance Europe'. *Journal of World History* 8: 1–27.

Headley, John M. (2000). 'Geography and Empire in the Late Renaissance: Botero's Assignment, Western Universalism, and the Civilizing Process' *Renaissance Quarterly*, 53: 1119–55.

Heuer, Christopher P. (2019). *Into the White: The Renaissance Arctic and the End of the Image*. New York: Zone Books.

Hitzel, Frédéric. (2010). 'Les ambassades occidentales à Constantinople et la diffusion d'une certaine image de l'Orient'. *Comptes rendus des séances de l'Académie del Inscriptions et Belles Lettres*, 1: 277–92.

Hodorowich, Liz. (2005). 'Armchair Travelers and the Venetian Discovery of the World' *Sixteenth Century Studies* 36: 1039–62.

Hung-kay-Luk, B. (1977). 'A Study of Giulio Aleni's "Chih-fang wai chi"'. *Bulletin of the School of Oriental and African Studies*. London: University of London: 40, 58–84.

Hunt, Alan. (1996). *Governance of the Consuming Passions: A History of Sumptuary Law*. Basingstoke: Macmillan.

Ikegami, Eiko. (2005). *Bonds of Civility*. Cambridge: Cambridge University Press.

Ilg, Ulrike. (2004). 'The Cultural Significance of Costume Books in Sixteenth Century Europe'. In Catherine Richardson, ed. *Clothing Culture 1350–1650*. Aldershot: Ashgate: 29–48.

Jacob, Christian. (1992). *L'Empire des Cartes. Approche théorique del la cartographie à travers l'histoire*. Paris: Albin Michel.

Jacob, Christian. (2006). *The Sovereign Map*. Chicago: Chicago University Press.

Jardine, Lisa, and Brotton, Jerry. (2000). *Global Interests, Renaissance Art between East and West*. Chicago: University of Chicago Press.

Johannesson, Kurt. (1991). *The Renaissance of the Goths in Sixteenth Century Sweden: Johannes and Olaus Magnus As Politicians and Historians*. Berkeley: University of California Press.

Katani Noriko. (2010). *Studies in Jesuit Art in Japan*. PhD dissertation, Princeton University. UMI Number: 3410891

Kato, Naomi (ed.). (2004). *Seiyo-Runessansu no Fashon to Seikatu*. Tokyo.

Kazutaka Unno. (1994). 'Cartography in Japan'. In Brian S. Harley and David Woodward, eds. *The History of Cartography*, vol. 2, *Cartography in the Traditional East and East Asian Societies*. Chicago: University of Chicago Press: 346–477.

Kovesi Killerby, Katherine. (2002). *Sumptuary Law in Italy, 1200–1500*. Oxford: Oxford University Press.

Krekich, Barisa. (1997). *Dubrovnik: A Mediterranean Urban Society, 1300–1600*. Ashgate.

Kundak, Ali Nihat. (2009). *An Ottoman Album of Drawings with European Engravings*. Thirteenth International Congress of Turkish Art Proceedings, Géza Dávid-Ibolya Gerelyes, eds. (Budapest, 3–8 September 2007). Budapest: Hungarian National Museum.

Kynan-Wilson, William. (2017). Painted by the Turks Themselves: Reading Peter Mundy Ottoman Costume Album in Context'. In S. Babaie and Mary Gibson, eds. *The Mercantile Effect: Art and Exchange in the Islamicate World during the 17th and 18th Centuries*. London: Ginko Library Art Series.

Leibsohn, Dana, and Favrot Peterson, Jeanette (eds.). (2012). *Seeing across Cultures in the Early Modern World*. London: Routledge.

Lestringant, Frank. (2005). 'Le volcan des glaces: de l'Histoire du septentrion d'Olaus Magnus aux Histoires prodigieuses de Pierre Boaistuau'. In *L'imaginaire du volcan* [online]. Rennes: Presses Universitaire de Rennes. http://books.openedition.org/pur/30838

Liddell, Jill. (1989). *The Story of the Kimono*. New York: Penguin.

Lieberman, Victor. (2009). *Strange Parallels: Southeast Asia in Global Context 800–1830*, vol. 2. *Mainland Mirrors: Europe, Japan, South Asia and the Islands*. Cambridge: Cambridge University Press.

Loh, Joseph F. (2013). 'When Worlds Collide: Art, Cartography, and Japanese Namban World Map Screens'. PhD diss. Columbia University.

Manners, Ian (ed.) (2007). *European Cartographies and the Ottoman World 1500–1750. Maps from the Collection of O. J. Sopranos*. The Oriental Institute of the University of Chicago: Oriental Institute Museum Publications no. 27.

Masayuki Sato. (1996). 'Imagined Peripheries: The World and Its People in Japanese Cartographic Imagination'. *Diogenes* 173(Spring): 44–63.

Masters, Bruce. (2016). 'Christians in a Changing World'. In Suraya N. Faroqhi, ed. *The Cambridge History of Turkey*. Cambridge: Cambridge University Press: 13, 272–80. http://universitypublishingonline.org/cambridge/histories

Mendes Pinto, Maria Helena. (1993). *Biombos Namban. Namban Screens*. Lisboa: Museu Nacional de Arte Antiga.

Mentges, Gabriele. (2007). 'Pour une approche renouvelée des recueils des costumes de la Renaissance: Une cartographie vestimentaire de l'espace et du temps'. *Apparence(s)* [en ligne], 1. http://journals.openedition.org/apparences/104. https://doi.org/10.4000/apparences.104

Miekkavaara, Leena. (2008). 'Unknown Europe: The Mapping of the Northern Countries by Olaus Magnus in 1539'. *Belgeo* (online)3–4: 307–24. http://journals.openedition.org/belgeo/7677

Miyoshi, Tadayoshi. (1993). 'Japanische und europäische Kartographie vom 16.bis zum 19.Jahrhundert'. In *Japan und Europa 1543–1929*. Berlin: Argon: 37–55.

Moran, J. F. (1993). *The Japanese and the Jesuits: Alessandro Valignano in Sixteenth-Century Japan*. London: Routledge.

Mukerji, Chandra. (2013). 'Costume and Character in the Ottoman Empire: Dress As a Social Agent in Nicolay's *Navigations*'. In Paula Findlen, ed. *Early Modern Things: Objects and Their Histories, 1500–1800*. London: Routledge: 151–69.

Nenzi, Laura. (2008). *Excursions in Identity: Travel and the Intersection of Place, Gender, and Status in Edo Japan*. Honolulu: University of Hawaii Press.

Newton, Stella M. (1988). *The Dress of the Venetians: 1495–1525*. London: Scholar Press.

Nordin, Jonas M., and Ojala, Carl-Gosta. (2018). 'Collecting, Connecting, Constructing: Early Modern Commodification and Globalization of Sami Material Culture'. *Journal of Material Culture* 23: 58–82.

North, Michael (ed.). (2010). *Artistic and Cultural Exchanges between Europe and Asia, 1400–1900: Rethinking Markets, Workshops and Collections*. London: Ashgate.

Olian, Jo Anne. (1977). 'Sixteenth-Century Costume Books'. *Costume Society of America* 3: 20–48.

Oliveira e Costa, Joao Paulo. (2004). 'Japan, Portugal and the World'. In Miyeko Murase, ed. *Turning Point: Oribe and the Arts in Sixteenth Century Japan*. New York: Metropolitan Museum of Art: 50–65.

Owen Hughes, Diane. (1983). 'Sumptuary Laws and Social Relations in Renaissance Italy'. In John Bossy, ed. *Disputes and Settlements: Law and*

Human Relations in the West. Cambridge: Cambridge University Press: 64–99.

Paulicelli, Eugenia. (2008). 'Mapping the World. The Political Geography of Dress in Cesare Vecellio's Costume Books'. *The Italianist* 28: 24–53.

Paulicelli, Eugenia, and Clark,Hazel. (eds.). (2009). *The Fabric of Cultures: Fashion, Identity, and Globalization*. London: Routledge.

Pedani, Maria Pia. (2010). *Venezia porta d'Oriente*. Bologna: Il Mulino.

Peirce, Leslie P. (1993). *The Imperial Harem: Women and Sovereignty in the Ottoman Empire*. New York: Oxford University Press.

Pitelka, Morgan. (2013). 'The Tokugawa Storehouse: Ieyasu's Encounters with Things'. In Paula Findlen, ed. *Early Modern Things*. London: Routledge: 297–315.

Pratt, Mary Louise. (1992). *Imperial Eyes: Travel Writing and Transculturation*. London: Routledge.

Proust, Jacques. (1997). *L'Europe au prisme du Japon, XVIe–XVIIe siècles*. Paris: Albin Michel.

Quataert, Donald. (1997). 'Clothing Laws, State and Society in the Ottoman Empire, 1720–1829'. *International Journal of Middle East Studies* 29(3): 403–25.

Raby, Julian. (2007). *The Serenissima and the Sublime Porte: Art in the Art of Diplomacy 1453–1600*. In Brahim Alaoui, ed. *Venice and the Islamic World 828–1797*. New Haven, CT: Yale University Press: 91–139.

Raby, Julian. (2017). 'Contents & Contexts: Re-viewing the Diez Albums'. In Julia Gonnella, Friederike Weis, and Christoph Rauch (eds.). *The Diez Albums: Contexts and Contents*. Leiden: Brill: 15–51.

Reichert, Folker E. (1993). 'Zipangu – Japans Entdeckung im Mittelalter'. In *Japan und Europa* 1543–1929. Berlin: Argon: 25–36.

Reolon, Giorgio. (2021). *Cesare Vecellio*. Il Prato.

Riello, Giorgio. (2019). 'The World in a Book: The Creation of the Global in Sixteenth Century European Costume Books', *Past and Present* supplement 14: 281–317.

Riello, Giorgio, and McNeil, Peter (eds.). (2010). *The Fashion History Reader: Global Perspectives*. London: Routledge.

Romano, Antonella, (2013). 'La prima storia della Cina. Juan Gonzales de Mendoza fra l'Impero spagnolo e Roma'. *Quaderni Storici* 142: 89–116.

Ropp, Paul S. (2010). *China in World History*. New York: Oxford University Press.

Rosenthal, Margaret F. (2007). 'Fashion, Costume, and Culture in Two Early Modern Illustrated Albums'. In Maurizio Rippa Bonati and Valeria Finucci, eds. *Mores Italicae: Costume and Life in the Renaissance*. Cittadella: Biblos: 79–108.

Rosenthal, Margaret F., and Jones, Ann Rosalind (eds.). (2008). *Cesare Vecellio's Habiti Antichi et Moderni: The Clothing of the Renaissance World*. London: Thames & Hudson.

Ross, Andrew C. (1994). *A Vision Betrayed: The Jesuits in Japan and China 1542–1742*. Edinburgh: Edinburgh University Press.

Ross, Robert. (2008). *Clothing: A Global History*. Cambridge: Polity Press.

Rothman, Natalie. (2009). 'Interpreting Dragomans: Boundaries and Crossings in the Early Modern Mediterranean'. *Comparative Studies in Society and History* 51: 771–800.

Rothman, Natalie. (2012a). *Brokering Empire: Trans-imperial Subjects between Venice and Istanbul*. New York: Cornell University Press.

Rothman, Natalie. (2012b). 'Visualizing a Space of Encounter: Intimacy, Alterity, and Trans-imperial Perspective in an Ottoman-Venetian Miniature Album'. *Osmanlı Araştırmaları: The Journal of Ottoman Studies* 40: 39–80.

Rothman, Natalie. (2021). *The Dragoman Renaissance: Diplomatic Interpreters and the Routes of Orientalism*. New York: Cornell University Press.

Roxburg, David J. (1995). 'Heinrich Friedrich von Diez and His Eponymous Albums: Mss. Diez A. Fols. 70–74', *Muqarnas* 12: 112–36.

Roxburg, David J. (2001). *Prefacing the Image: The Writing of Art History in Sixteenth-Century Iran*. Leiden: Brill.

Roxburg, David J. (2005). *The Persian Album, 1400–1600: From Dispersal to Collection*. New Haven, CT: Yale University Press.

Rublack, Ulinka. (2010). *Dressing Up: Cultural Identity in Renaissance Europe*. Oxford: Oxford University Press.

Schick, Leslie M. (2004). 'The Place of Dress in Pre-modern Costume Albums'. In Suraya Faroqhi and Christoph K. Neumann, eds. *Ottoman Costumes: From Textile to Identity*. Istanbul: Eren: 97–116.

Schmidt, Benjamin. (2011). 'Collecting Global Icons: The Case of the Exotic Parasol'. In Daniela Bleichmar and Peter C. Mancall, eds. *Collecting across Cultures*. Philadelphia: Pennsylvania University Press: 31–57

Schulz, Juergen. (1987). 'Maps As Metaphors: Mural Map Cycles of the Italian Renaissance'. In David Woodward, ed. *Art and Cartography: Six Historical Essays*. Chicago: Chicago University Press: 97–122.

Screech, Timon. (2002). *The Lens within the Heart: The Western Scientific Gaze and Popular Imagery in Later Edo Japan*. Honolulu: University of Hawaii Press.

Screech, Timon. (2011). *Obtaining Images: Art, Production and Display in Edo Japan*. Chicago: University of Chicago Press.

Shintaro Ayusawa. (1964). 'Geography and Japanese Knowledge of World Geography'. *Monumenta Nipponica*, 19:275–94.

Shively, Donald. H. (1964–5). 'Sumptuary Regulation and Status in Early Tokugawa Japan'. *The Harvard Journal of Asiatic Studies* 25: 123–64.

Strunck, Christina. (2003). *Identità vere e finte nel programma decorativo del palazzo di Bassano. Albani, Domenichino, Tempesta, Castello e Guidotti dipingono per Vincenzo Giustiniani*. In Agostino Burreca, ed. *La villa di Vincenzo Giustiniani a Bassano Romano*. Rome: Ministero per i Beni e le Attività Culturali, Soprintendenza per i Beni Architettonici per il Paesaggio e per il Patrimonio Storico Artistico e Demo etnoantropologico del Lazio.

Sullivan, Michael. (1989). *The Meeting of Eastern and Western Art*. Berkeley: University of California Press.

Tagliaferro, G., and Aikema, B. (2009). *Le botteghe di Tiziano*. Florence: Alinari.

Tetsuo Najiita. (1987). *Visions of Virtue in Tokugawa Japan*. Chicago: University of Chicago Press.

Toby, Ronald P. (1998). 'Imagining and Imaging "Anthropos" in Early Modern Japan'. *Visual Anthropology Review* 14: 19–44.

Toby, Ronald P. (2001a). 'Rescuing the Nation from History: The State of the State in Early Modern Japan'. *Monumenta Nipponica* 56: 127–237.

Toby, Ronald P. (2001b). 'Three Realms/Myriad Countries: An Ethnography of Other and the Re-bounding of Japan, 1550–1750'. In Kai Wing Chow, Kevin Michael Doak, and Poshee Fu, eds. *Constructing Nationhood in Modern East Asia*. Ann Arbor: University of Michigan Press.

Todorova, Maria. (1997). *Imagining the Balkans*. New York: Oxford University Press.

Tracy, James D. (1990). *The Rise of Merchant Empires: Long-Distance Trade in the Early Modern World*. Cambridge: Cambridge University Press.

Tranberg Hansen, Karen. (2004). 'The World in Dress: Anthropological Perspectives on Clothing, Fashion and Culture'. *Annual Review of Anthropology* 33: 69–92.

Traub, Valerie. (2000). 'Mapping the Global Body'. In Peter Erickson and Clark Hulse, eds. *Early Modern Visual Culture: Representation, Race and Empire in Renaissance England*. Philadelphia: University of Pennsylvania Press: 44–92.

Tremml, Birgit M. (2012). 'The Global and the Local: Problematic Dynamics of the Triangular Trade in Early Modern Manila' *Journal of World History* 23: 555–86.

Tuffal, Jacqueline. (1955). 'Les recueils de costumes gravés au XVI siècle'. In *Actes du I Congres Internationale d'Historie du Costume*. Venise: 262–9.

Um, Nancy, and Clark, Leah. (2016). 'The Art of Diplomacy: Situating Objects and Images in the Early Modern Diplomatic Encounter'. Special issue of *Journal of Early Modern History*, 20: 1.

Valensi, Lucette. (1987). *Venise et la Sublime Porte*. Paris: Hachette.

Valensi, Lucette. (1990). 'The Making of a Political Paradigm: The Ottoman State and Oriental Despotism'. In Anthony Grafton and A. Blair, eds. *The Transmission of Culture in Early Modern Europe*. Philadelphia: University of Pennsylvania Press: 173–203.

Van Groesen, Michiel. (2008). *The Representations of the Overseas World in the De Bry Collection of Voyages (1590–1634)*. Leiden: Brill.

Venturi, Lionello. (1957). *Bibliotheque Pillone*. Paris: Pierre Berès.

Wang Gungwu. (2008). 'The China Seas: Becoming an Enlarged Mediterranean'. In Angela Schottenhammer, ed. *The East Asian 'Mediterranean': Maritime Crossroads of Culture, Commerce and Human Migration*. Wiesbaden: 7–22.

Wigen, Karen. (2010). *A Malleable Map*. Berkeley: University of California Press.

Wilson, Bronwen. (2004). 'Reproducing the Contours of Venetian Identity in Sixteenth Century Costume Books'. *Studies in Iconography*, 25: 221–74.

Wilson, Bronwen. (2005). *The World in Venice: Print, the City, and Early Modern Identity*. Toronto: University of Toronto Press.

Wilson, Bronwen. (2007). 'Foggie diverse di vestire de "Turchi": Turkish Costume Illustration and Cultural Translation'. *Journal of Medieval and Early Modern Studies*, 37: 99–139.

Wodianka, Stephanie. (2015). 'Localisation de l'art: conceptions d'une 'esthétique du froid' de l'Histoire des Peuples du Nord (Olaus Magnus, 1555) au Tasse (Il Re Torrismondo, 1587)'. *Babel. Littératures Plurielles* 32: 129–58.

Woodward, David. (1996a). 'The Camocio Atlas'. James Ford Bell Lectures, University of Minnesota. http://bell.lin.unm.edu/wood.htlm

Woodward, David (1996b). *Maps As Prints in the Italian Renaissance: Makers, Distributors and Consumers*. The 1995 Panizzi Lectures. London: British Library.

Woodward, David. (2007). *The Italian Map Trade, 1480–1650*, in David Woodward, ed. *The History of Cartography*, Vol 3. *Cartography in the European Renaissance*. Chicago: University of Chicago Press: 779–91

Woolf, Larry. (2002). *Venice and the Slavs: The Discovery of Dalmatia in the Age of Enlightenment*. Stanford, CA: Stanford University Press.

Yonemoto, Marcia. (2003). *Mapping Early Modern Japan*. Berkeley: University of California Press.

Acknowledgements

In the course of my research, I presented parts of this work at a number of talks and seminars and I would like to thank all participants for their questions, input, and attention: colleagues and doctoral students in the Department of History and Civilization at the European University Institute in Florence, Ulinka Rublack in Cambridge, Albert R. Ascoli and Barbara Spackman in the Department of Italian Studies at the University of California (Berkeley); Paula Findlen and our graduate students in the Department of History at Stanford; Susanna Burghartz at the University of Basel; and Cornelia Aust, Thomas Weller, and Denise Klein in Mainz. Anthony Molho, Catherine Bond, Tommaso Munari, and Martin Kohli read parts of this Element. Martin's collection of ancient travelogues and costume books in Berlin offered me unending suggestions and fun.

A special mention goes to Constanta Vintila and the research team of the ERC-funded project Luxury, Fashion and Social Status in Early Modern Southeastern Europe, Grant agreement ID: 646489 at New Europe College in Bucharest that hosted talks and seminars for five intense years of collective work, and where parts of this research were presented and discussed. Dr Mario Talamo translated all texts from Chinese and Japanese. Dr Simona Di Marco guided me through the wealth of the Stibbert Library and Museum.

I thank the editors of the series: John Henderson who invited me to join and Jonathan Nelson for his careful reading of the entire Element and for his acute insights.

I dedicate this Element to Martin.

Cambridge Elements

The Renaissance

About the Series

Timely, concise, and authoritative, Elements in the Renaissance showcases cutting-edge scholarship by both new and established academics. Designed to introduce students, researchers, and general readers to key questions in current research, the volumes take multi-disciplinary and transnational approaches to explore the conceptual, material, and cultural frameworks that structured Renaissance experience.

Cambridge Elements

The Renaissance

Elements in the Series

Paradoxes of Inequality in Renaissance Italy
Samuel K. Cohn, Jr

The World in Dress: Costume Books across Italy, Europe, and the East
Giulia Calvi

A full series listing is available at: www.cambridge.org/EREN

Lightning Source UK Ltd.
Milton Keynes UK
UKHW020738150922
408910UK00009B/996